Anthony Gunn is a psychologist whose personal experience with phobias began when he underwent emergency surgery without anaesthetic in Honduras. The experience left him with a debilitating fear of medical procedures, but through his training he overcame his own phobia and now helps others deal with theirs. He gives regular talks and radio interviews about phobias, and has written articles for magazines. For more information go to fearispower.com.au

Fix your phobia in 90 minutes

Vermilion

LONDON

1 3 5 7 9 10 8 6 4 2

Published in 2011 by Vermilion, an imprint of Ebury Publishing
First published in Australia by Penguin Group in 2009

Ebury Publishing is a Random House Group company

Copyright © Anthony Gunn 2009

Anthony Gunn has asserted his right to be identified as the author of this
work in accordance with the Copyright, Designs and Patents Act 1988.

The Random House Group Limited Reg. No. 954009

Addresses for companies within the Random House Group can be found
at www.rbooks.co.uk

A CIP catalogue record for this book is available from the British Library

The Random House Group Limited supports The Forest Stewardship
Council (FSC), the leading international forest certification organisation.
All our titles that are printed on Greenpeace approved FSC certified
paper carry the FSC logo. Our paper procurement policy
can be found at www.rbooks.co.uk/environment

Mixed Sources

Product group from well-managed
forests and other controlled sources
www.fsc.org   Cert no. TT-COC-2139
© 1996 Forest Stewardship Council

Printed and bound in the UK by
CPI Cox & Wyman, Reading, RG1 8EX

ISBN 9780091939656

Copies are available at special rates for bulk orders. Contact the sales
development team on 020 7840 8487 for more information.

To buy books by your favourite authors and register for offers, visit
www.rbooks.co.uk

Contents

To my loving parents, Ron and Helen Gunn,
who taught me to believe in myself.

Introduction

If you've bought this book to overcome a phobia, rest assured that you are in good company. Phobias can affect anyone, regardless of their income, social status or intelligence. It's been estimated that as many as one in four people live with a phobia.

Although there are literally hundreds of phobias – everything from a fear of heights, spiders or public speaking to a fear of eggs, shadows or even string – they can be classified into three basic categories:

- Specific phobias: fear of a specific object or situation, such as animals, needles, water, flying or heights

- Agoraphobia: fear of open spaces
- Social phobias: fear of negative evaluation from others, such as when eating, writing or speaking in public

Of the three, specific phobias respond best to the 90-minute treatment described in this book. Agoraphobia and social phobias can also be treated using the same principles, though it generally takes longer.

If you are thinking that your phobia is different and will not respond to treatment, research shows that any specific phobia can be treated, regardless of the age it began, its severity and whether there is a history of phobias in your family. What is most important is how *determined* you are to overcome your phobia, and also how diligently you follow the steps in this book.

There are endless misconceptions about the causes and treatment of phobias. Can you relate to any of the following?

- 'People with phobias are obviously attention seekers because their fear is so irrational.'
- 'To get rid of a phobia you just need to ignore it.'
- 'Phobias are caused by chemical imbalances in the brain.'
- 'Only medication can help a phobia.'
- 'Phobias indicate a lack of intelligence and/or a weak personality.'

Over the next ten chapters, I will show you that none of these statements is true, and instead, give you the tools to overcome your phobia. It's crucial that you *read each chapter* – don't skip over any – and that you take the time to complete the practical exercises. Even if you feel an exercise isn't necessary for your situation, it's important to discipline yourself to do it anyway, and to keep practising it. Each exercise gives you another skill that you'll need for your 90-minute treatment. In the same way that a professional athlete trains before a main event, you are training yourself to confront your phobia. Every time you complete an exercise, you are indirectly tackling your phobia.

In the first chapter I will show you how a phobia gets stronger every time you avoid it, and in later chapters you will see that when you beat avoidance, a phobia comes crashing down like a house of cards.

But *Fix Your Phobia* is not only useful for people with phobias; it is also a great resource for family and friends who want to assist them. Living with a phobic person can be difficult. Not knowing how to help them and having to alter your own life to accommodate someone else's phobia can be frustrating. If you want to help someone face their phobia, your role as a support person or 'phobia friend' is vital. I discuss this in detail in Chapter 7.

You can face a phobia in one of two ways: gradually over a period of weeks, or rapidly in 90 minutes. Think of removing a band-aid. You can do it slowly and it will painfully remove one hair at a time. Or you can pull it off quickly, with only minor and brief discomfort. Both methods achieve the same results. By choosing the rapid approach, you will do more than successfully treat your phobia – you will also learn some amazing skills that can be applied to other challenges in your life.

1
You're not weird!

What is a phobia?

Phobias are incredibly common, and anyone can get them. But what exactly *is* a phobia? Put simply, it's a strong, involuntary fear of a particular object or situation. The fear reaction is irrational because it is way out of proportion to the actual danger the object/situation presents. People with a phobia will usually completely avoid the object/situation (called a 'phobic stimulus'), or endure it with intense distress.

The degree to which a phobia disrupts your life generally depends on the ease with which you can avoid your phobic stimulus. For example, it is a lot easier to avoid snakes if you live in the city as opposed to the country. Yet, in the city it is a lot harder to avoid elevators, tunnels and heights.

Specific phobias can be grouped into five categories:

- Animal/insect phobias: fear of spiders, snakes, birds, bees, dogs etc.
- Natural environment phobias: fear of heights, storms (e.g. thunder, lightning, tornadoes), rivers, the ocean, waterfalls etc.
- Phobias of blood and/or medical procedures.
- Situational phobias: fear of airplanes and other forms of transport, elevators, tunnels, bridges, enclosed spaces etc.
- All other rare phobias: fear of choking, vomiting, contracting an illness, cotton balls, balloons, buttons, fish tanks, feathers, paper with holes in

it, the number 13, loud or unpleasant
sounds (e.g. fingernails on
chalkboard), costumed characters etc.

Disgust or fear?

Certain phobias may make a person feel more
disgusted than afraid. This is most common with
phobias of spiders, rats, bees, snakes or blood.
People with this sort of phobia feel so disgusted
when exposed to their phobic stimulus that they
experience nausea and may vomit. The feeling of
disgust, though physically different from fear, still
triggers avoidance and the attendant unpleasant-
ness and difficulties of a phobia. Throughout this
book, when I refer to a phobic response, I mean
disgust as well as fear.

Who gets phobias?

Betsy had a phobia of heights that prevented
her from doing a whole range of things,
including going for job interviews in

multistorey buildings, visiting anyone in a two-storey house, holidaying in multistorey motels and driving over bridges. Betsy often had vivid nightmares involving heights. Aside from her phobia, Betsy had a completely normal life. She was intelligent, quick-witted, caring and had a great sense of humour. Even with all these positive attributes, however, Betsy felt like a failure because she could not overcome her phobia. She had resigned herself to believing she was mentally weak.

Like Betsy, do you believe that only weak people have phobias? Successful people who are strong, disciplined and mentally tough would not be susceptible to having phobias, right?

WRONG!

Phobias can affect anybody, whether they are a renowned scientist, international celebrity or ordinary person. If you don't believe me, take a look at the list below.

You're not weird!

....

Andre Agassi (tennis champion)	arachnophobia (fear of spiders)
Muhammad Ali (boxing champion)	aviophobia (fear of flying)
Napoleon Bonaparte (military leader)	ailurophobia (fear of cats)
Charles Darwin (explorer, writer)	hematophobia (fear of blood)
Agnetha Faltskog (ABBA star)	acrophobia (fear of heights)
Sigmund Freud (psychiatrist)	ornithophobia (fear of birds)
Alfred Hitchcock (film director)	ovophobia (fear of eggs)
Harry Houdini (magician)	claustrophobia (fear of confined spaces)
Nicole Kidman (actress)	mottephobia (fear of moths/butterflies)
Madonna (singer)	brontophobia (fear of thunder)
Ronald Reagan (former US president)	aviophobia (fear of flying)
Donald Trump (entrepreneur)	chirophobia (fear of shaking hands)
Andy Warhol (Pop artist)	nosocomephobia (fear of hospitals)

How common are phobias?

Phobias are the most common psychological problem there is. They are estimated to affect anywhere from 10 to 25 per cent of the population, though it's hard to get precise figures because so many people avoid treatment. Phobias are also the easiest problem to treat, yet they often go undiagnosed because people prefer to alter their lives to avoid their phobia rather than seek treatment. Do you know anyone who you suspect has a phobia, but has never sought help for it? There are plenty of clues in people's everyday behaviour. Here are some examples:

- Aunt Mary cannot look at pictures of spiders.
- Fred the local mechanic will not travel in elevators or enter confined spaces.
- Colin, a gym instructor, refuses to climb ladders or stand on anything high, and becomes angry and aggressive if you push him on this.

- Grandma cannot stand balloons and will not allow them in her house.
- Toby proudly tells others that the only way anyone would get him on a plane would be in a coffin.

Why do people avoid seeking help?

In my experience, many people with phobias believe that nothing can be done to treat their problem because it is part of who they are – they are 'just born that way'. Others live in denial about their phobia, ashamed to admit that they even have one, let alone talk about the extent of the suffering and inconvenience it causes them. They will often aggressively defend their position by stating things like, 'It is *not* a problem. I just do not like [insert phobic stimulus here], *okay*?!' The one thing that *all* people with phobias have in common is avoidance. Take Bob, for example:

Bob came to see me to treat his phobia of caterpillars. On the day of his appointment, Bob got to the front door of my office, but then the fear of confronting his phobia kicked in and he hurried straight back to his car and drove away. Bob later phoned to apologise for not keeping his appointment, and explained that his fear got too much and that the only way he knew to get rid of it was to escape the situation. On his second attempt, Bob was able to make it through the door and together we started fixing his phobia.

The problem with the avoidance strategy is that it actually *strengthens* your phobia. When you can take ownership of your phobia, the closer you will be to conquering it.

> *People with phobias have a*
> *'black belt' in avoidance.*

How can you be sure you have a phobia?

Given that there are so many people with unrecognised phobias, how can you tell if you have a real phobia as opposed to simply having a strong fear of a specific object or situation?

To determine whether you have a phobia you need to ask yourself the following simple questions:

- When faced with your feared object or situation (phobic stimulus), do you have an immediate fear response (sweating, shaking, palpitations, dizziness) that is severe enough to interfere with your daily life?
- Do you come up with elaborate ways to avoid your phobic stimulus, or else endure it with intense distress?
- Does merely thinking about the thing you fear make you anxious?
- Do you dread the next possible encounter with your phobic stimulus?

- Does the avoidance, anxious anticipation or distress in the feared situation interfere significantly with your normal daily functioning?
- Are you aware that your fear is excessive or unreasonable in response to your phobia, but feel that you are unable to control it?

If you answered 'yes' to question 6 and to at least four of the other questions, then it is highly likely you have a phobia. Question 6 is crucial because a person with a phobia can acknowledge to themselves that their fear is excessive and unrealistic, but they still feel powerless to do anything about it.

If you answered 'no' to more than two of the above questions, then it is likely you have a strong fear rather than a phobia. Even so, the principles in this book will still be of great benefit to you.

You're not weird!

....

> **NOTE FOR PARENTS:** If you have a child under 18 and suspect that they have a phobia, then their fear towards the phobic stimulus must have been present for **at least** six months before you should consider treatment. This is because children develop strong fears towards a variety of things, but then quickly outgrow them.

Identifying a phobia is an important step – the first blow to your phobia's armour. By bringing it out of hiding and labelling it as something that can affect anyone, you take away some of its power. You see, phobias are all about *control*, or rather, lack of control. If your phobia is the boss you are likely to feel that:

- You do not have any control over your own reaction.
- Your phobia is unique to you.
- You are mentally weak for having a phobia in the first place.
- Nothing can be done about it.

> *Feeling weak for having a phobia only strengthens it.*

The Little Devil

Imagine that your phobia is a little devil sitting on your shoulder telling you why you should not treat it.

> Mark had a bee phobia, but was able to identify what the little devil on his shoulder was whispering to him about the pitfalls of treatment. The little devil was telling him:
>
> - You won't be able to cope.
> - The psychologist will trick you into doing things you don't want to do.
> - You'll have a heart attack.
> - You're weak for having the phobia in the first place.
> - Nothing can be done about it.
> - You'll only make a fool of yourself.

The 'little devil' metaphor is very useful in helping people with phobias identify the untruths going through their mind about treatment. One of the most common of these is the fear of being tricked. Every person with a phobia that I have treated has had the same worrisome question about treatment, 'Will I be thrown in at the deep end?' For example:

> Rachel had a phobia of confined spaces.
> I explained to her that anyone can develop a phobia; I outlined what would and would not happen during treatment, and we established the benefits she could expect to gain from treatment. Yet Rachel remained sceptical, thinking she would be tricked into doing something against her will. Her 'little devil' kept telling her that she would be forced into a small room and remain locked in there until her phobia was gone.

This idea of being thrown in at the deep end with your phobia in order to treat it is known in psychology as 'flooding'. This will *not* happen in your 90-minute program for a very important reason: it would deprive you of a sense of control – a vital element in the process of overcoming your phobia. In the coming chapters you will be learning some powerful psychological techniques that will foster this sense of self-control.

Flooding has another major drawback: it can go horribly wrong and *reinforce* your phobia.

Peggy had a phobia of crickets and her friend decided to help her beat it by introducing a container of them to her without warning. Peggy saw the crickets and leapt backwards so violently that she broke her foot. Peggy then associated the injury with the crickets, further reinforcing her phobia.

Okay – enough with the devil. Now imagine that on your other shoulder there's a dejected angel worn out from trying to tell you why you need to conquer your phobia and all the reasons why treatment *will* work, but to no avail. How can you help? The key is to turn up the volume on the angel's voice simply by listening to it. And the more attention you pay to the angel, the more its words will overpower the devil's.

> Ray's little angel told him that if his phobia of birds was fixed, he would be able to travel (so many cities and beach locations have seagulls, pigeons and other birds), visit zoos and animal sanctuaries, live in a house instead of a flat, hang the clothes out during the day instead of at night, and simply be able to walk about comfortably without always looking out for birds. It also told him that the treatment would work, and that afterwards he'd be more confident in public and have much higher self-esteem.

Now you know that phobias can affect anyone and that every time you *avoid* your phobia, including denying having one at all, you are reinforcing it. Remember, the moment you can openly and honestly acknowledge your phobia instead of feeling weak for having it, you are on your way to taking on its strength as your own. You become the master and your phobia becomes the servant.

Exercises

1. On a piece of paper, **write down the pros and cons** of treating your phobia – get to know both your little devil and your little angel.

    For the **cons**, ask yourself:

    - What am I afraid of?
    - What is the little devil telling me about what will happen during treatment?

    For the **pros**, ask yourself:

    - What will I be able to do that I can't do now?
    - Where will I be able to go?

16

- How will my self-esteem change?
- How will my behaviour change?
- What else will be different in my life?

2. Keep reminding yourself that **phobias can affect anyone**. Look for other people living with a phobia. Search the internet for celebrity phobics and/or phobia chat sites; and ask people around you if they know of others who have a phobia. You will be amazed at what you uncover.

2

Phobias are learned

Barry had a crippling phobia of storms that
prevented him from travelling, going outside
on overcast days and even getting to sleep on
a rainy night. No matter what Barry did to try
to fix his phobia, he could not get rid of it. He
tried a multitude of remedies such as carrying
healing crystals in his pocket to fend off bad
karma, changing his diet, and taking
medication prescribed by his doctor. Barry
resorted to alcohol when he had to take a
plane flight, even if the potential for flying
through bad weather was slight. Barry
believed that he was born with his phobia,

and that nothing could be done to get rid of it. He resigned himself to having to avoid any situation where the weather looked remotely like triggering his phobia.

Can you relate to Barry's dilemma? What do you think triggered your phobia? Was it because of a past event or do you think it is innate? Obviously, nothing can be done for your phobia because you were born with it, right?

WRONG!

Phobias are *learned*, which is great news because it means they can be *un*learned.

Generally, phobias are childhood fears we've never outgrown, but they can also develop in adulthood. Many parents unknowingly keep their children's phobias alive by preventing their kids from facing and mastering the situation that scares them. In a similar way, phobias can be passed down through families via modelling, or other learning styles – but they're *not* passed down genetically.

Jane had a phobia of mice. When she was a child, her family home had a short period of mice troubles. One day Jane was in the bath when a mouse ran under the bathroom door and looked up at her. Jane screamed and the terrified mouse ran around in circles, unable to find its way out. Because the mouse was between Jane and the door, she could not escape either. Added to this, Jane had locked the door, so her parents could not get in to help her. Eventually her father picked the door's lock and killed the mouse. From that time on, anything to do with mice – pictures of mice, mouse droppings or even someone saying the word 'mouse' – caused Jane to react hysterically. As a result, Jane's family went out of their way to shelter her from any kind of encounter with mice.

Psychologists have shown that phobias like Jane's are not only learned, but that the original phobic stimulus can expand to include similar things or events. For example, Jane's phobia of mice ended up mutating to the point that she could not stand to see or touch *anything* that was small, furry and grey including toys, folded socks and even dust rags. If your phobia has mutated like Jane's, by concentrating on fixing the main phobia you will help fix its offshoots. Remember, your aim is to stay focused and target your main phobia first.

In some cases, however, it is harder to access the main phobia (especially fear of flying in an airplane, storms and lightning) so you may have to treat the offshoot or a secondary phobia first. For example:

Ruth's husband wanted her to go scuba diving with him, but she had a phobia of water. (Her water phobia developed after she nearly drowned in the bath when her long hair was sucked down the plughole.) The thought of going in the ocean was horrifying to her, and the idea of having a diving mask over her face sent chills down her spine. Not only was Ruth terrified by water, but she also feared confined spaces, and felt trapped with any sort of mask on her face. Ruth's secondary phobia of confined spaces prevented her from even putting on the equipment to treat her phobia of water so she could go diving. It was easier to treat her phobia of confined spaces than her fear of water and scuba diving. Once her fear of confined spaces was successfully treated, the confidence she'd gained and the strategies she'd learned could be transferred to her fear of scuba diving.

Here's another example:

Arnold had a phobia of flying. On one occasion he and his wife had checked in for a flight and were about to walk up the external staircase to board the plane. But the steps triggered Arnold's phobia of heights. Arnold, a solid and tall man, then became fearful that being in a small cabin so high above the ground could make him lose control of himself and injure either himself or others. Neither Arnold nor his wife boarded the plane and they forfeited their tickets. In this case Arnold's secondary phobia (his fear of heights) was easier (and cheaper) to access than his primary phobia (his fear of flying). The confidence and strategies he gained in overcoming his fear of heights were then transferred to enable him to overcome his fear of flying.

If you have more than one phobia, target the main one or the one that is most easily accessible.

Why can't I remember where my phobia came from?

Many people cannot remember any specific incident that might have triggered their phobia, which suggests that the phobia was developed during infancy or early childhood, prior to the onset of memory formation. By contrast, the part of the brain responsible for processing fear has the ability to 'remember' fear from as early as nine months of age. This makes it possible for a fearful childhood experience to be stored before any conscious memory of the event was recorded. For example:

> Graham, a man in his forties, has a phobia of dogs. A few years ago his parents told him that his dog phobia might have something to do with him being bitten by a dog when he was 18 months old. Graham has no recollection of the event and questions whether it really caused his phobia.

The good news is that Graham does not have to know the origins of his phobia to successfully treat it in 90 minutes, and neither do you.

Knowing where your phobia came from is not essential to treating it.

So why doesn't my phobia just go away?

A phobia remains in control of you *because you allow it to*. Believing you were born with your phobia is one way of letting the phobia maintain its hold over you. However, it is not the only way. Other ways your phobia stays strong are through you physically avoiding it, and using medication, drugs and/or alcohol to numb your feelings.

Physical avoidance

Physical avoidance is any action you perform to escape the situation or thing you are afraid of (your phobic stimulus). It can mean steering clear of touching it, not wanting to be in the same place as it, and not being able to look at it.

> Katrina employed all three avoidance techniques towards her phobia of rats. She would never touch anything that resembled a rat, including small furry animals and stuffed toys. Likewise, she would not walk past places

where rats might live, such as rubbish bins,
alleyways, sewers or drains. She could not
even look at a picture of a rat, so whenever a
rat appeared on television, Katrina would
look away until her husband told her it was
safe to look again.

The problem with physical avoidance, or any form
of avoidance for that matter, is that it not only
prevents you from learning that you can manage
the fear associated with your phobia, but also *fuels*
your phobia. For example:

Imagine it is late at night and your car is the
only one left in a car park. As you approach
the car you reach for your keys, only to
discover that they are not in your pocket.
Instantly you react with fear and have the
horrible thought that you have lost them. As
you search frantically through your bag, your
head fills with fearful images of what could
happen to you if you can't get home. Then,

> when all seems lost, you suddenly find the
> keys buried at the bottom of your bag.

If you can relate to this scenario then you may also be able to relate to the relief you feel upon finding the keys – it's as if a huge weight has been lifted from your shoulders. A phobic person will experience a similar feeling of relief when they narrowly avoid being in contact with their phobia. The problem is that this feeling is like a reward, which means that the avoidance behaviour will be repeated, further strengthening the phobia.

Medication

Some people will go to their local doctor and be prescribed medication to fix their phobia. The idea that a phobia is caused by a chemical imbalance in the brain only supports the misconception that people are born with phobias.

> Brian had a phobia of choking on food, which
> crippled his life. His doctor prescribed

> medication to calm him down before he ate.
> The problem was that not only did the
> medication make Brian lose his appetite,
> but he felt dependent on it.

Medication works by suppressing, and hence avoiding, the feelings of fear associated with confronting the phobia. The problem with this band-aid solution is that once the medication wears off, the phobic feelings return. The result is that you take another pill and the cycle continues without you ever having addressed the main issue, namely that the phobia is *learned*.

NOTE: Medication can be beneficial for certain mental illnesses. However, when the single presenting issue is a phobia as outlined in this book, research shows medication to be counterproductive.

Specific phobias can occur with mental disorders, but research shows that when specific phobias develop in this context, they tend to be much less severe than the original mental disorder. In such cases, the mental disorder needs to be treated first.

Examples of mental disorders that might precede the development of a specific phobia are:

- panic disorder (especially for height and claustrophobia)
- depression

Drugs and alcohol

Drugs and alcohol are a form of self-medication which, like any medication, may temporarily subdue a phobia, but often with unhealthy side effects. These include the increased risk of addiction and withdrawal symptoms once the drug of choice has worn off. Added to this, the diminished control over actions while under the influence of drugs and/or alcohol can make people more vulnerable to further harm.

> Sandra got a job as a photographer for a local newspaper, but had a phobia of horses. As she was based in a farming community, Sandra would often have to go to horse studs to get

photos for upcoming stories. To conceal her phobia from others (and herself), she would smoke marijuana to calm herself down prior to a visit to a horse stud. Unfortunately, the quality of Sandra's photos was then far below her usual standard and she lost her job.

Every time you avoid your phobia,
you reinforce it.

How phobias are learned

Stanley Rachman, an expert research psychologist, says people learn phobias in three ways:

- direct personal experience
- watching other people
- sharing information

Direct personal experience

As we have seen, the most common way for a phobia to develop is after a traumatic event. A person learns to associate that event (or an element of it) with potential danger and develops a phobia of it.

> Tamara's phobia of possums developed many years ago when she was in a hurry to bring her cat in one night. Absentmindedly she picked up what she thought was the cat eating out of the cat-food dish but, to her horror, it turned out to be a possum. Now Tamara will not go anywhere at night for fear of being attacked by a possum, and she bursts into tears if she sees one. Even talking about possums makes her cringe.

Examples of phobias that might develop after direct personal experience include:

- Fear of driving after being in a car accident.
- Fear of bees after being stung by one.
- Fear of needles after fainting while giving blood.

To 'unlearn' your phobia you will utilise the power of direct personal experience. Now before you close the book in terror, rest assured that I will guide you through all the preparation you need to do before you are ready to face your phobia. For now, know that to conquer any phobia, especially in 90 minutes, learning through direct experience is vital. This is why other so-called phobia 'cures' such as healing crystals, hypnotism, dietary changes and thinking happy thoughts have not been proven to fix phobias.

Watching other people

For many people, watching someone else being afraid or having a negative experience in a certain situation has taught them a phobia. This form of learning is powerful because it utilises the psychological learning principle called 'modelling'. People learn more from others' actions than from their words – something many parents overlook.

Examples of phobias that might develop after watching someone else's experience include:

- Watching the movie *Jaws* and not being able to swim at a beach.
- Repeatedly watching a parent with a phobia and now having the same, or a similar, phobia.
- Seeing television images of the September 11, 2001, terrorist attacks and being afraid of flying.
- Watching a friend experience an allergic reaction after being stung by an insect and subsequently refusing to go outside in summer for fear of being stung too.

To unlearn your phobia, you will also use modelling by recruiting a trusted 'phobia friend' to help you face your phobia. This will happen much later (Chapter 7), but for now, you can feel secure in the knowledge that you will not be expected to face your phobia alone.

Sharing information

Phobias can also be learned through sharing information about a fearful object or situation. (For example, someone could have a phobia of worms without ever having touched one.) Such information is spread through books, magazines, newspapers, movies, TV, rumours, the internet, radio or just listening to people recall their experiences.

Unfortunately, the media are masters at sharing fear-provoking information and they capitalise on people being drawn to stories about terrorism, shark attacks, child abduction, plane and road accidents, crime, murder, epidemic diseases, road rage, killer insects and animals, earthquakes, storms … the list goes on.

Examples of phobias that might develop from shared information include:

- Hearing of someone being caught in a traffic jam when driving through a long tunnel and developing a phobia of tunnels.

- Watching a news story about a shark attack and developing a phobia of swimming in the ocean.
- Reading a magazine article about mistakes that can happen during surgery and developing a phobia of hospitals.

To fix your phobia, you will be taking in all the new information I give you in this book – especially the skills you learn by completing each chapter's exercises. Likewise, you will absorb only information that helps to conquer your phobia, not information that reinforces it. You will not behave like Larry, for example, who had a phobia of flying but loved reading articles and watching TV shows on plane crashes.

Is your phobia more like a 'combo deal'?

If you feel that your phobia is the result of more than one form of learning, then you're probably right. For example:

Sarah had a phobia of leeches, though she
could not attribute just one of the three
learning methods outlined above as the main
cause. Firstly, Sarah saw the 'leech scene' in
the movie Stand By Me, where the young boy
faints after finding a blood-filled leech.
Watching this scene repulsed Sarah,
especially when her friend, who was watching
the movie with Sarah at the time, incorrectly
explained that leeches keep sucking a
person's blood until there is no blood left.
A few weeks later Sarah went on a short
bushwalk. During the walk she was
confronted with the unimaginable: a leech on
her shoe. Instantly recalling the movie's leech
scene and her friend's comment about
leeches never being satisfied, Sarah ripped off
her shoe and threw it over a cliff. As a result
she had to walk home with only one shoe,
panicking the whole time that a leech might
find her unprotected flesh. Years on, Sarah
refused to go bushwalking, would not look at

pictures of leeches in books or on TV, and
when anybody started talking about leeches
she would leave the room.

Sarah developed her phobia of leeches through a
combination of the three learning methods. When
used in the right way, these three methods can
also be used to unlearn a phobia. In the following
chapters you will face small challenges ('exercises')
unrelated to your phobia that will teach you how
to manage fear, gradually breaking your old learning patterns and instilling new ones.

Exercises

- **Learn from personal experience**:
  try a new food or go somewhere you
  would not normally go.
- **Learn from others**:
  think of something you have always
  wanted to do (dance, sing, paint,
  grow your own vegies …) and see a

performance, exhibition or workshop
where someone else is doing it.

- **Learn from media information:**
  listen to or read inspirational stories of
  people who overcame great adversity
  and let this motivate you to continue
  on your journey of facing your phobia.

3

The power of emotion

Elizabeth's phobia of spiders was so strong that she looked away when a spider appeared on television. She could not touch a plastic spider or even look at a picture of a spider in a book. Whenever spiders were talked about in detail, Elizabeth would refuse to listen. She knew her phobia was irrational, but felt she could not beat it. Her husband, family, friends and work colleagues all told her that she should be able to just get over it, as no one could be that scared of spiders unless they were just after attention.

People generally hate their phobia because it makes them react in embarrassing ways and limits their quality of life. However, when I tell people that their phobia is a gift, offering an amazing opportunity for learning, they look at me as if I am completely loony. After all, if a phobia has been limiting a person's life, at times even crippling it, then it has absolutely no value, right?

WRONG!

Your phobia is far from worthless because of its *emotional* connection. Few situations in everyday life (apart from birth and death experiences) can elicit the emotional reaction of a phobia. And it is precisely this intensity that you will learn to manage when you fix your phobia – a process that you can then apply to other situations in your life.

Think back to the time you broke up with your first boyfriend or girlfriend. Now think about what you had for dinner two Saturdays ago. Can you even remember? Events that are linked to emotions, like a relationship break-up, are far more memorable than everyday events, like eating dinner. This is why you only need to experience a high-emotion event once to remember it, compared to the constant repetition needed to recall facts.

To highlight how powerful emotions can be, see if you can recall the following events:

- Buying your first car
- Having a mental blank in an exam
- Princess Diana's death
- Your child being born
- September 11, 2001

Were you able to recall all of the events above? If not, it could suggest that some of them were not emotionally charged for you. Take a short break and recall an event that is both personal and highly memorable for you, and think about how you felt at the time. Try to think of an event that triggered negative emotions such as fear or grief. Most people are terrified of experiencing intense emotions, so to avoid triggering them they will remain prisoner to their old behaviour patterns. Successfully facing your phobia in 90 minutes involves first learning to manage high-intensity emotions in a controlled environment. By being able to accept and sit with powerful feelings, you will be able to take control of your reactions to your phobic stimulus and other challenges.

The main obstacle that will prevent you from mastering the powerful emotions associated with your phobia is seeing them as a weakness.

Why do we see emotions as a weakness?

Many people are terrified of experiencing strong emotion because they feel totally out of control.

Darrel's fiancée called off the wedding just weeks before the big day. Darrel was devastated, but whenever anyone asked how he was, he assured them that everything was fine. To try to prevent himself from fully

> experiencing his emotions, Darrel began to
> drink heavily and withdraw from people.
> Eventually he came to counselling, which
> allowed him to drop his guard and cry.
> Darrel had been scared of lowering his guard
> because he thought he might lose control
> forever. Yet he was surprised to find that not
> only did he not lose control, he also felt that a
> huge weight had been lifted.

Viewing the expression of emotion as a weakness is fuelled by the misconception that success is based on *not* feeling. When the action hero fights the bad guy, we assume they do so without being 'limited' by their emotions. Likewise we usually hear the confident assertions of athletes before they compete, never their fears. This implies that if you feel or show any emotion, then you are weak and inadequate.

But how do people avoid feeling? One way is by avoiding situations that may trigger emotions – in particular watching other people expressing theirs. This is why people often discourage others from expressing certain emotions. Can you recognise any of the following?

- 'Real men don't cry.'
- 'Cut your losses, forget it and move on.'
- 'Don't worry, there are plenty more fish in the sea.'
- 'Just ignore her – she's like that to everyone.'
- 'There is always someone worse off than you.'

Why are emotions so hard to suppress?

When giving public talks, I demonstrate how emotionally driven humans really are, and how difficult it is to block these emotions. A volunteer from the audience is hooked up to a machine that measures sweat – a good indicator of fear. Next I introduce Ernie, a two-metre non-venomous

python, and ask the volunteer to touch him.
Upon seeing the snake, the volunteer's sweat/fear
levels skyrocket. I explain that Ernie is harmless
and the volunteer usually nods their head in
understanding, but their sweat/fear levels still rise.
I encourage the volunteer to suppress their fear,
but they are unable to do so. The more they try,
the more they sweat. This demonstration high-
lights that it is virtually impossible to suppress fear
– the key emotion triggered by a phobia.

Adam had to telephone his solicitor to
commence legal proceedings against his
neighbour, but the moment it came time to
make the call, he always seemed to become
distracted by a more pressing issue, like
checking emails or rearranging his work desk.
Once Adam completed the minor task, he
would go back for a second attempt at making
that difficult call. The pattern continued, with
Adam finding a new distraction each time he
sat down to make the call. Finally, at the end

> of the day, procrastination won out and Adam
> decided that next week would be a better time
> to call his solicitor.

What happened? Every time Adam went to call his solicitor, the feelings flooded in. The only way Adam knew how to deal with them was to avoid making the call. This avoidance is especially true for phobias. Are there certain things or places you avoid because they might trigger your phobia? In fact, *it is not the situation that you are avoiding, but rather your emotional response to it.*

We like to think of ourselves as logical thinkers who can suppress any unwanted emotions. Yet, rational thinking is merely the tip of the iceberg when it comes to motivation. Much of the time we are motivated to act the way we do by our feelings. Expecting logic to override emotion is like expecting a mouse to hold down a lion. Accepting that emotions motivate you, and that they cannot be controlled with logic, is the first step to managing them.

If you ask yourself why you chose your partner, your home, your work, your car and even
your clothes, it is likely that your reasons were not
practical, but rather emotional. Yet we continue
to believe that to be victorious in any endeavour,
we must push emotions to the side. As a psychologist, I find it frustrating that many people think
that they can help someone 'get over' an emotionally charged phobia by simply talking it away with
common sense.

Why can't phobias be talked away with common sense?

When a well-wishing person attempts to help
someone conquer their phobia, the first and usually
only self-help technique they offer is common
sense. Their approach is based on using plain facts
to show the person with a phobia that they are
over-reacting and that there is nothing to worry
about. Can you relate to any of these pearls of
wisdom that many people think will cure an
emotionally charged phobia?

- 'You have more chance of being hit by lightning than being bitten by a shark. So don't worry, just get in the water.'
- 'Flying is perfectly safe. You have far more chance of being killed in a car accident than a plane crash, and you drive your car every day.'
- 'You have lived 38 years of your life without being stung by a hornet. Therefore the chance of you being stung today is less than 1 in 13879!'
- 'If you were hit by a car travelling at 50 km/h, it would be similar to falling from a five-storey building. Just tell yourself that if you can walk across a busy road, then you can climb a ladder.'

Instead of helping, this type of advice usually makes you feel even weaker and more helpless for not being able to out-think your phobia. Look at this example:

Steve developed a phobia of ceiling fans after his father teased him as a child that they could fall from the ceiling and chop him up. As a result, Steve would avoid walking into rooms with ceiling fans, and would never walk under one. The more that people told Steve there was nothing to fear from ceiling fans, the worse he felt about not being able to beat his phobia. Steve knew that his phobia was irrational. He also knew that if it were that easy to beat a phobia by talking it away with common sense, he wouldn't have a phobia in the first place.

People cannot talk away a phobia using logic because phobias are learned in the part of the brain called the amygdala – which is off-limits to facts and so-called common sense. The only language that the amygdala, and therefore a phobia, understands is the language of emotions. Trying to cure a phobia by talking logic to it is a bit like explaining something in Japanese to someone who speaks only Greek.

To be able to conquer your phobia in 90 minutes, you need to be completely fluent in the language of emotions – this means you need to be able to *accept* your emotions and to learn to 'sit' with them. This is quite a challenge because, subconsciously, most people believe that avoiding emotions will actually protect them from pain. This is a normal response and something we need to treat with respect.

To lower the defences that prevent you from experiencing emotions, you are going to take small, planned steps. The first step is to *accept as normal* any feelings brought on by the idea of treating your phobia (including any fear brought on while reading this book).

That is all you have to do to take your first step. If you can recognise your emotions and see them as completely normal, then you are engaging them. The more you do this, the easier it will be to sit with your emotions instead of trying to avoid them.

Learning to 'sit' with emotions

By 'sitting' with emotions, I mean noticing when you are feeling nervous or afraid or disgusted and then being able to *observe* the feeling without automatically reacting to try to get rid of it. Think of it like riding a wave. At first a wave rears up strongly and seems as if it could dump and pummel you, but the longer you ride it, the smaller and weaker it becomes, until finally it reaches the shore a fraction of its original size and strength. The same happens with intense emotions. If you can *surf* the discomfort associated with your intense emotions, then, like the wave, its intensity will drop very quickly.

> Fran tripped over in the shopping centre and skinned her knees. She was fine, but felt terribly embarrassed. Weeks later, whenever Fran thought back to the event she would physically cringe and try to stop herself thinking about it. But of course the more she tried to push the memory away, the stronger it

seemed to become. Instead of running from the memory of her embarrassment, Fran was taught to surf the feeling by observing it without reacting. Even though it was initially quite intense, Fran was amazed at how quickly the discomfort dropped, and was equally amazed at the positive effect it had on her self-esteem.

Exercises

To face your phobia in 90 minutes it is vital that you get to know your emotions. The following exercises are designed to help you achieve this by doing uncomfortable activities that are unrelated to your phobia. Some of the exercises may seem unusual, but you must *do them anyway*. Do each exercise in your own time. The aim is for you to identify any feelings you have, and to simply observe them.

- Have a drink of something, but at the wrong temperature (e.g. a cold cup of

tea or coffee, or a warm glass of
water). How do you feel?

- Watch a comedy show on TV that you
  know usually cracks you up, but do
  not allow yourself to laugh for a short
  period of time (e.g. 10 minutes).
  Then allow yourself to laugh and
  notice how different it feels.

- Take your shoes off and gently
  massage your own feet. Notice how
  it feels.

- Bite into a segment of lemon or run
  your fingernails down a chalkboard.
  Notice how strongly your emotions
  try to prevent you from performing
  these actions.

- When alone, scream into a pillow as
  loud as you can. How did you feel
  afterwards?

- Skip for a short distance or take a ride
  on a swing in a park. How did you
  feel afterwards?

- Rent a 'tear-jerker' movie and allow
  yourself to cry. (If you're not sure
  which films might qualify, ask at your
  video store.) Notice how you may
  initially try to stop yourself from
  crying – but let go. The experience is
  eye-opening, and you can do it alone
  if you find this easier.

How did you go? Did you desperately want to
stop what you were doing to avoid your discomfort, or were you able to sit with your emotions,
accepting and observing them without judge-
ment? If you had trouble letting go, have a short
break and try the exercises again later. Fortu-
nately, emotions come naturally and *anyone* can
learn to let them flow. So stick with it. You are
already on the road to mastering your emotions,
and ultimately, your phobia!

4

Up close and personal

> Rob desperately wanted to travel overseas,
> but his needle phobia meant he couldn't go to
> the countries he wanted to because he could
> not get the vaccinations. He tried pills,
> potions, diets, crystals and self-help CDs,
> and paid large sums of money to various
> gurus who promised a permanent cure –
> all to no avail.

There are many optimistic, well-wishing people
who genuinely believe that a person can get rid of

their phobia forever. After all, if a phobia is learned and can be unlearned, it makes sense to assume that a successfully treated person is forever cured, right?

WRONG!

You cannot 'get rid of' a phobia permanently. Scientists have discovered that when a phobia is learned, it is 'burnt' into the amygdala – the part of the brain responsible for identifying fears – and cannot be undone. However, the brain can be *reprogrammed* to respond differently to that fear, and that's what this book is all about. A fixed phobia is a bit like a muzzled Doberman on a lead: the dog is still there, but it is under its master's control.

Now, before you put this book down in despair, be aware that you can use your phobia's stubbornness to your advantage. A successfully treated phobia will become your own motivational coach whenever you face fearful situations. I explore this in Chapter 10.

People are lured towards expensive remedies that claim to cure phobias with the promise of a 'fear-free treatment' – in other words, without them having to be exposed to the object or situation that they are afraid of. This is quite simply avoidance, and as you will recall from Chapter 2, avoiding a phobia is what keeps it strong and powerful.

Warren developed a phobia of moths after one flew into his ear while he was out jogging one night. The moth buzzed around in his ear canal and Warren went to hospital to have it removed via a simple procedure. Years later, the scars of that experience remained. Warren wanted to get rid of his moth phobia, but without having to face a moth or his feelings about them. First he tried taking a very expensive natural herb, which promised to cure all phobias in a week. He continued taking the herb for an extra week, thinking he had not followed the instructions properly. When this did not work, he tried the promised 'six-session phobia cure' using hypnosis.

After five sessions nothing had changed, but Warren still prayed that somehow the sixth session would make it all come together and cure his phobia. His prayers went unanswered. He continued to try a variety of 'fear-free' remedies and therapies that all promised the same outcome. Sadly for Warren's self-esteem and his bank balance, none worked.

If someone promises to cure a phobia without exposure, it's a scam.

To manage your phobia you will need to get up close and personal with your phobic stimulus, to befriend it. But before you can do that, you need to understand what triggers your avoidance behaviour. You see, it's your avoidance that keeps your phobia strong, and prevents you from getting to know your phobic stimulus in detail. Most people with a phobia think that they know their phobic stimulus really well, especially since it has ruled their life for so long, but research actually shows the opposite. When tested, most people know very little about the object or situation that they fear – they've spent so many years avoiding it, how could they have accrued any facts? For example:

- A person with a phobia of bats might never have actually seen one, so could not accurately describe the features of a bat.
- A person with a phobia of confined spaces is unlikely to be able to describe what the inside of a walk-through aquarium looks like.
- A person with a phobia of balloons is likely to have never actually touched an inflated one.

After successfully facing his height phobia, Ryan was amazed at what he saw when looking over a four-storey balcony. Previously he had been so preoccupied with escaping the situation that looking at the scenery was the last thing on his mind.

The more you can take the mystery out of your phobia, the less power it will have over you. To take control of your phobia you first need to understand how it has controlled you. It does this by triggering automatic avoidance behaviour, which I call 'safety behaviour'.

How do you respond to your phobia?

Safety behaviour is any action performed automatically to protect yourself from danger. For example, if something is thrown towards your face, you will close your eyes and turn your head away – you don't think about it, you simply do it. This is *helpful* safety behaviour, as it genuinely protects you. However, safety behaviours associated with a phobia are *unhelpful* because they promote avoidance, thereby strengthening your phobia. Examples of phobia safety behaviours include:

- Looking away, running away, having a panic attack, becoming hysterical or bursting into tears when potentially encountering your phobic stimulus.
- Coming up with excuses to avoid facing your phobic stimulus.
- Becoming angry or aggressive when someone challenges you about facing your phobic stimulus.

Phobia safety behaviours do not harm you directly; in fact, their intentions are good because their aim is to protect you from perceived danger. The problem is that the more effective they are in stopping you from facing your phobic stimulus, the stronger your phobia becomes.

So how do you respond to your phobic stimulus? And what safety behaviours automatically kick in? Take the time, now, to write down your answers to the following questions.

*1. What do you do when potentially faced with
the object or situation you are afraid of?*
Do you, for example:

- Look away?
- Scream and run?
- Freeze up, too terrified to move, and
  endure it with great distress?
- Pass out? (This usually only applies to
  phobias of blood, injury and
  injections.)

*2. What goes on in your mind when you are
potentially faced with the object or situation you
are afraid of?*
Knowing how to deal with phobic thoughts will
be covered in Chapter 6, but for now I want you
to identify the types of thoughts that are going
through your head. Do you, for example, tell
yourself that you are going to:

- Die?
- Suffocate?

- Pass out?
- Vomit?
- Lose control of your bowels?
- Panic?
- Feel humiliated or embarrassed?

3. *What is your body's physical reaction to your phobic stimulus?*

In Chapter 8 I'll show you how to deal with these bodily symptoms, but for now it's important that you identify what happens to you physically when you potentially face your phobic stimulus. Do you experience:

- Racing or pounding heart?
- Breathlessness or feelings of being smothered?
- Dizziness or light-headedness?
- Difficulty swallowing – a choking feeling or 'lump' in the throat?
- Shaking?
- Chest pain or tightness in the chest?

- Nausea or diarrhoea?
- Crying?
- Sweating?
- A dry mouth?
- Hot flushes or chills?
- Blurred vision?
- Numbness and tingling?
- Tightness or weakness in the muscles
  (e.g. jelly legs, sore neck)?
- Uncontrollable nervous laughter?
- A trembling or cracking voice?
- Blushing?
- 'Butterflies' in the stomach?
- Poor concentration (e.g. forgetting
  what you are trying to say)?
- A feeling of unreality or being
  detached?

How close can you get?

Write down what will trigger your phobia safety behaviours. Some people do not even need to be near their phobic stimulus to experience the behaviour, thoughts and physical reactions listed above. For example, some people react to:

- Smells
- Words, pictures or television/movie scenes
- Similar objects (such as socks triggering a mouse phobia)
- People simply talking about their phobic stimulus (e.g. a needle)
- Imagining their phobic stimulus

Other people have varying degrees to which they can approach their phobic stimulus. For example, a person with a phobia of:

- Heights – may be able to stay in a room and look out at the balcony but not step onto the balcony.
- Confined spaces – may be able to stand at the door of an elevator but not walk in.

- Animals – may be able to watch their feared animal from 50 metres away, or as little as 5 metres away as long as it is behind a barrier (e.g. a secure fence).
- Needles – may be able to look at a syringe or even hold it, but never watch someone have an injection or have one themselves.

Knowing how close you can get before your phobia safety behaviours kick in will allow you to establish a physical baseline to work from. This baseline will become your starting point, or safety zone, from where you will take small, planned steps towards facing your phobia in Chapter 9.

If you do not know how close you can comfortably get to your phobic stimulus, try this experiment. Find a safe and controlled situation with a clear exit. For example, if you have a phobia of:

- Dogs – you could approach a *friendly* dog that is behind a high and secure

fence and then estimate, or have a
friend measure, your distance from
the dog.

- Spiders – you could approach a spider
  outside in its web or on a wall and then
  estimate, or have a friend measure,
  your distance from the spider.
- Heights – you could walk towards the
  edge of a lookout or high balcony and
  determine how close you can get to
  the edge.
- Confined spaces – you could walk into
  or get as close as possible to a safe,
  confined space and have a friend
  measure either how close you get, or
  how long you are able to stay in there.
- Rats – you could approach a pet rat in
  a cage and measure how close you can
  get to the cage.

Your goal is to establish your *safety zone* – the
distance you can manage being from your phobic
stimulus.

Rate your phobia

To determine the level of discomfort you are experiencing when facing your phobia, you will need to rate it using the Phobia Fear Scale. This is a simple score out of 10, where 0 represents no discomfort at all (i.e. completely relaxed and unafraid), and 10 represents the worst discomfort imaginable (i.e. mortal terror). Only reserve a 10 rating for an absolutely horrific fear response – I am yet to treat a person for a phobia who got to 10 during the treatment process.

You will use the Phobia Fear Scale throughout your own 90-minute treatment. It will be like a thermometer, proving through gradual increments that your 'fear temperature' is coming down.

Get to know your phobia

As we have seen, most people with a phobia do not really know much about the situation or thing they are afraid of, due to avoidance triggered by phobia safety behaviours. As a result, their minds fill in the blanks and make the fear worse.

> During her treatment, Katrina was shocked to
> discover that not only do rats have rabbit-like
> buck teeth on their top and bottom jaws
> (instead of fangs as she once thought), they
> also have little claws rather than the sharp
> talons she'd been imagining for years. Katrina's
> phobia of rats had prevented her from ever
> observing a rat in detail. Her phobia was based
> on fleeting glimpses and her vivid imagination.

Katrina developed the following short checklist during her treatment to educate herself about her rat phobia:

Questions I have about rats	Beliefs I held before treatment	What I learned
What do its eyes look like?	They are small and beady	They are round and cute-looking
What do its teeth look like?	Like dog's teeth with big fangs	A bit goofy, like a rabbit's or a guinea pig's teeth
What do its ears look like?	Sharp and pointy	Soft and rounded

Questions I have about rats	Beliefs I held before treatment	What I learned
What do its feet look like?	Sharp claws with razor-like talons	Just small claws – not talons
What does its fur feel like?	Stiff and wiry	Soft like baby hair

These are only examples, though similar questions could be applied to any phobia. For example, with a phobia of heights, possible questions to broaden your awareness could include:

- What can you see along the horizon?
- What can you hear?
- Can you see any birds or clouds?
- Can you identify any objects below?
- How different do these objects look compared to how you previously saw them?

Stress is phobia fertiliser

Stress plays a powerful role in feeding phobias. Not only can it fuel the intensity of a phobia, it can also bring a previously dormant phobia to life.

Nigel was in his mid-forties when he developed a phobia of heights. This was a major problem for him because he was a construction worker specialising in multistorey buildings. Nigel came to me because he could not explain why, after years of being able to walk along scaffolding hundreds of metres above the ground, he'd suddenly developed a fear of heights.

After talking with Nigel, I discovered that he had many stressors in his life. He was going through a divorce after his wife had had an affair. His mother had recently died, his work was going through a slow period, the bills were piling up, his son was being bullied at school, and Nigel's trusty work companion of over fourteen years, Spud, a blue cattle dog,

became sick and had to be put down. Nigel
had dismissed all the stress in his life by using
the common but very harmful saying, 'There
are people worse off than me.'

To treat Nigel's height phobia we first had
to tackle the stress. Nigel consulted legal and
financial experts to help with his divorce and
money worries. He spoke with the school staff
and got their support in dealing with the
bullying of his son. And finally, Nigel took
time out for himself by using an array of
relaxation and other self-care strategies.
Once this stress was reduced, we were able to
work on quickly treating his phobia.

Though self-care strategies will not directly fix a
phobia, they are useful in decreasing underlying
stress that could be fuelling it. I thoroughly
recommend yoga, massage and exercise to help
reduce or better deal with the stress in your life.
But this does not mean that you should move to
the hills and live like a monk. In our fast-paced

society, it is virtually impossible to avoid stress, and you wouldn't want to any way – it's important for our survival. However, you *do* have a say in how much stress you take on. The only way you will know how much stress is in your life is by becoming aware of the way your body responds to it. Even though stress is different from discomfort, you can still use the principle of the Phobia Fear Scale to rate your response to it. Whether your stress is being fuelled by work or home life, rating it gives you a sense of control where you previously felt none.

Exercises

1. **Practise using the Phobia Fear Scale** whenever you come across a fear-provoking situation unrelated to your phobia, no matter how small. If you have to deal with a difficult person or child, rate it; if you have to drive the car under stressful conditions, rate it; if you have to make a customer complaint, rate it.

The more you are able to rate your fear responses, the more you will get to know them, and the more you will feel that you can manage them, including the fear associated with your phobia.

2. **Develop a checklist of things to observe** when you confront your phobia (see Katrina's example earlier). The more creative and unique your questions, the better. The whole aim of the checklist is to make you aware of features you previously would not have noticed or deliberately avoided noticing. By making yourself aware of these traits about your phobia, your mind can focus on different aspects and hence help break the automatic cycle of avoidant behaviour.

3. **Start educating yourself**. If you have a phobia of a specific animal, read all you can about its behaviour and habits. If you fear being in tunnels, read up on how they are

designed and built. If you fear medical procedures, learn how the body works and how it repairs itself. Whatever your phobic stimulus, become an expert on it.

5

Build your
mind fitness

> Marsha had a phobia of eggs that began when
> she once cracked an egg open on her breakfast
> plate to find a dead chick inside. From then
> on, Marsha felt physically sick whenever she
> saw an egg. This discomfort was so strong
> that she avoided any contact with eggs, not
> even allowing them in her house.

Often when a person is faced with a situation or
event involving their phobia, it causes such intense
discomfort that all they want to do is avoid it. If

this discomfort is so awful and so disruptive to a normal life, it makes perfect sense to try to eradicate it, right?

WRONG!

Psychologists now know that trying to avoid uncomfortable feelings sparked by a phobia will only make things worse. Why? Because avoidance empowers your phobia. If you can *sit* with the discomfort, it drops very quickly and allows you to get around phobia safety behaviours.

As you learned in the previous chapter, safety behaviour is anything you automatically do to avoid confronting your phobic stimulus (the thing you are afraid of). But this behaviour is not triggered by the phobic stimulus itself, but by the *feelings of discomfort* (nausea, panic, sweating etc) that you associate with it. It might be hard to accept at first, but trust me – it is not the phobic stimulus that you fear; rather it's your reaction to it. People will go to great lengths to try to avoid feeling this discomfort.

Tracy had a phobia of cockroaches. If a person even started talking about cockroaches she felt like she was going to vomit, and would quickly race out of the room. This happened at her son's wedding, when the best man retold a harmless practical joke involving the groom and a cockroach. Upon hearing the start of the story, Tracy bolted from the room, creating an embarrassing scene.

*It's not the spider you are afraid of,
but your reaction to the spider.*

Phobia safety behaviours are powerful. This is why the technique of facing a phobia head-on rarely works – our phobia safety behaviours will simply not allow it to happen. Remember, their job is to protect you from perceived danger. Therefore the more potential discomfort you put yourself in – i.e. facing your phobia head-on without any preparation – the harder your safety behaviours will work at making you avoid the situation, and prevent you from facing your phobia.

The key to getting around phobia safety behaviours is to sit with the feelings of discomfort that trigger them.

> Tracy could not say the word 'cockroach' due to the discomfort she felt, yet she took on the challenge of saying the word as fast as she could (faster was easier) for 30 seconds, the whole time accepting her discomfort and surfing it out. To Tracy's surprise, her discomfort dropped very quickly and by the end of the 30 seconds she could say the word 'cockroach' slowly without reacting.

Yet, surrendering to discomfort in order to gain self-control may well seem counterintuitive. A common misconception is that to conquer a phobia, you need to be able to feel that you can control the thing that scares you. In other words, you need to be able to control that which is external to you; namely, your phobic stimulus. This could not be further from the truth. You do not have full control over *anything* external to you.

The only thing you have full control over is your own reaction.

Marsha made herself walk into a room where there was an egg sitting on a table. She focused on controlling her own reaction (she wanted to run out of the room) instead of trying to control the egg by wishing it was not there. This change in focus brought Marsha closer towards overcoming her phobia.

Look at the list below and see if you can identify the avoidance behaviour that occurs when people try to control their phobic stimulus instead of focusing on controlling their discomfort to it.

- Getting your house regularly sprayed to try to control a phobia of spiders

and/or insects (the spiders/insects
eventually come back again).

- Hanging clothes on the line at
  night-time to try to control a phobia
  of birds.
- When going up or down stairs,
  walking as close to the wall as possible
  to try to control a phobia of heights.
- Taking a long detour to avoid driving
  through a tunnel to try to control a
  phobia of confined spaces.
- As a fearful passenger on a plane,
  wanting to check up on what the
  pilots are doing whenever there is an
  unusual noise or slight bit of
  turbulence.

In all of the examples above, the person is trying
to control the phobic stimulus instead of their
own reaction to it. Trying to control things that
are external to you in the hope that you will gain
control of yourself only brings disappointment.

Twelve-year-old Stephanie found this out the
hard way.

> Stephanie had a phobia of choking on food.
> She would always carefully check her food
> for lumps or any ingredient that might
> choke her. But one day a small chunk in her
> mashed potato got past Stephanie's guard at
> a special dinner with her family and friends.
> Even though not large or firm enough to
> cause any trouble, she instantly spat the
> potato out and embarrassed herself in front
> of her friends. By learning to focus on
> controlling her reaction to the food instead
> of trying to control the food itself, Stephanie
> was eventually able to face and then fix
> her phobia.

Learning to sit with discomfort

In order to sit with the discomfort associated with
your phobia, you first need to build up your

strength of mind. This is similar to building up your body's fitness: you start with lighter exercises and gradually build up the intensity. Many people, however, fall into the trap of thinking that they should be able to master any psychological skill instantly and they try to do too much too quickly. When training to conquer your phobia, overdoing any psychological exercise may destroy your confidence and turn you off for good, which Pamela discovered when she tried to fix her phobia of fish.

> Pamela felt so disgusted by fish that her phobia prevented her from not only eating them but also looking at pictures of them and even going into any shop or supermarket where fish were sold. Yet, after Pamela read about the psychological principle of accepting discomfort, she felt so confident and empowered that she went straight to the local fish shop to confront her phobia once and for all. However, the closer she got to the front door of the shop, the worse she felt.

> Eventually the feelings of discomfort became so intense that she ran back to the car in tears. Her confidence in tatters, she could not understand how she could be so confident one minute and then a blubbering mess the next. What happened? Pamela had tried to run a marathon on her first day of training and faced too much discomfort too quickly without building up to it.

To avoid falling into the same trap as Pamela, you will need to build up your mind strength gradually so that you become much more capable of sitting with discomfort. To do this, we'll use a little helper – chocolate! If you are unable to eat chocolate because of an allergy, you could try using a small knob of butter or a block of ice.

You will need:
- a few small squares of plain milk chocolate (or butter or ice)
- a comfortable chair
- a clock placed at eye-level

What to do:

1. Take one square of chocolate (or whatever you are using), place it on your tongue and close your mouth. Check the time.

2. Keep the chocolate there for two minutes. Sounds easy? Well, here's the challenge. Under no circumstances are you to react by swallowing, biting down, moving your tongue, lips, jaw, neck or head. Laughing is also out. *You must remain still for the whole two minutes.* It might help to keep your eyes closed at first.

3. Sit with the discomfort and rate it. First it will increase rapidly, and then just as quickly decrease.

NOTE: It is impossible to drown from a build-up of saliva in your mouth!

How did you go? Were you able to last the full two minutes? If you did, well done! I now encourage you to do it again, but for longer, say three minutes. If you were unable to do it then rest assured, you are normal. On their first attempt very few people last the whole two minutes without swallowing or reacting in some way. The key is regular practice. I urge you to keep repeating this exercise over several days until you have mastered the full two minutes. Once you have achieved this, keep pushing yourself by extending the time limit each go. The chocolate exercise is brilliant at teaching you to sit with discomfort, but without the real-life fear associated with facing your phobia.

> Tristan had a phobia of butterflies. After trying the chocolate exercise and then following the rest of the treatment steps in this book, he was amazed at how quickly the discomfort dropped when he forced himself to look at a photo of a butterfly.

The more you can master sitting with this discomfort, the more you will see that contrary to what your phobia safety behaviours are telling you, you have a *choice* in the way you react to your phobia. However, this all starts by focusing on controlling your *reaction* to your feared object or situation instead of trying to control the object or situation.

A NOTE OF CAUTION: In permitting yourself to feel discomfort, you are not expected to ignore danger, physical pain or bullying by another person. Your safety is of the utmost importance. Never let anyone compromise it.

Exercise

Do the chocolate exercise again, though this time use the Phobia Fear Scale you learned in Chapter 4 to assess your differing levels of discomfort. Sit with the discomfort and rate it. Notice how it initially increases, and then just as quickly starts to decrease.

6

Label your thoughts

In his youth, Ted and his friend watched the hit movie Jaws. Ted recalled that he was terrified, but peer pressure meant he watched the whole film. Twenty-seven years later, Ted still feels the effects of the movie and avoids the ocean for fear of sharks. Just thinking about sharks makes him break out in a sweat. On rare occasions, after being coaxed by friends, Ted has gone into the water up to his ankles, but then panics and runs out again. He believes that no matter how shallow the water is, a shark will be waiting to eat him because it knows how scared he is. Ted

acknowledges that his beliefs about sharks
are totally irrational, yet he cannot seem to
shake this negative thinking.

If simply *thinking* about a phobia can set it off,
then it makes sense not to think about it, and to
try to ignore such thoughts, right?

WRONG!

Phobic thoughts *cannot* be ignored. Ignoring
is avoidance, and as you have learned from the
past five chapters, *avoidance is what keeps a phobia
strong*. If you can do the opposite – i.e. *concentrate* on the phobic thoughts – they'll melt like
ice cream on a hot day. To learn how to concentrate on phobic thoughts, you first need to understand how phobic thoughts work.

What are phobic thoughts?

Phobic thoughts are the internal conversations
we have with ourselves about our phobia. Always
negative, biased, exaggerated and unrealistic, they

focus on avoiding perceived danger and will tell you *anything* to make you evade your phobia.

Of course, internal monologue is not limited to people with phobias. Psychologists use the term self-talk to describe the conversations we have with ourselves. It's estimated that the average person speaks to themselves at over 500 words per minute. A person's self-talk when faced with their phobia generally becomes more intense and fearful. This means that when you face your phobia, either in your mind or in real life, you will be hit by a barrage of intense and negatively charged thoughts.

Phobic thoughts are irrational because they use predictions instead of facts to make decisions. For example, logically Ian knew that he could walk into a room and stand under the light without the light-bulb exploding. However, Ian's phobia meant that he chose to ignore this fact and predicted, instead, that the light-bulb would explode and shower him in hot glass the moment he walked under it. With phobic thoughts, facts go out the window and irrational predictions rule supreme.

How do phobic thoughts distort your thinking?
All phobic thoughts are distorted in the same way, regardless of your particular phobia. They will always:

- overestimate a negative outcome
- underestimate your ability to cope

Overestimating the chance of something bad happening if you face your phobia is very common and helps to fuel the avoidance behaviour that keeps your phobia strong. Your phobic thoughts achieve this by using 'What if' statements, which overestimate a particular negative outcome. For example:

- 'What if I panic and cause an accident?'
- 'What if the bridge collapses when I drive over it?'
- 'What if while going for a walk I see a dog and it attacks me?'

Underestimating your ability to cope will devalue any successful confrontation you have with your phobia, lowering self-esteem and fuelling thoughts of a negative outcome.

> Max had a phobia of nylon. Either touching it or hearing pieces of nylon fabric rub together sent chills down his spine. Max had kept his phobia hidden, but his wedding day was fast approaching, and he was terrified that his bride-to-be might surprise him by wearing nylon lingerie on their wedding night. All he could think about was his wife's devastation at seeing his uncontrollable negative reaction. Max believed his reaction would cause his new wife to leave him, which would then lead to him having a nervous breakdown.

Even though the choice of words may vary from person to person, phobic thoughts always involve overestimating a negative outcome and underestimating our ability to cope. Other examples:

- **Spider phobia**:
  'Spiders know that I am scared of them and will not be happy until they push me to one day having a heart attack.'
- **Animal phobia**:
  'I seem to attract dogs/rats/snakes/sharks. They seek me out because they can smell my fear.'
- **Height phobia**:
  'If I get too close to the edge I will lose control and be pulled off the edge.'
- **Phobia of confined spaces**:
  'If I am trapped in a small room, the air will run out and I will die or have a mental breakdown.'
- **Needle phobia**:
  'I will totally flip out and lose control of myself when the needle goes in my arm, causing the needle to either go straight through my arm or break off in me.'

- **Storm phobia**:
  'If lightning is going to hit anyone, it
  will single me out because it knows I
  am scared and can't cope.'

Phobic thoughts feed on themselves

Phobic thoughts can easily escalate in both nega-
tivity and intensity. Think of them as a snowball
rolling down a steep mountain. The snowball
starts off small and as it gains speed and momen-
tum, it grows in size until it becomes an avalanche.
In a similar way, your phobic thoughts will grow in
strength the more you avoid facing them.

Avoiding phobic thoughts gives us false reas-
surance that we've prevented the worst from
occurring. This is why when many people confront
their phobia, they perceive it as a lucky escape
from danger rather than a victory. For example,
Stacey explains an encounter with her phobia of
centipedes:

'Being trapped in the bathroom with a centipede for nearly two hours was worse than death. I am just grateful that I was able to get out before the fear made me lose my mind.' Stacey was in contact with her phobia for over 90 minutes, the same amount of time it will take to face yours. Why did it not fix her phobia? Because she did not target her phobic thoughts, and as a result, tricked herself into believing that she'd barely escaped from the worst actually happening – a mental breakdown. End result: the perceived 'lucky escape' only served to strengthen her phobia of centipedes.

So if you cannot beat phobic thoughts by ignoring them, what do you do? You need to start *challenging* them, just a little, by identifying and labelling them as they arise. Remember, phobic thoughts retain their strength by being kept hidden.

Labelling your phobic thoughts is effective because it stretches your mind, breaking your usual reaction cycle so that you can see your thoughts for what they are. Whenever the human mind is stretched by thinking in a different way, it never goes back to its original shape. Think of the mind as being like a balloon. When you fill a balloon and then let the air out, the balloon will not go back to its original shape because it has been stretched. If you can label your phobic thoughts you will have challenged and 'stretched' them. Even the smallest stretch will prevent them from going back to their original shape and intensity.

Of course, before you can label your phobic thoughts, you need to be able to identify them.

How to identify phobic thoughts

Some people find it very hard to identify their phobic thoughts, especially if even thinking or talking about their phobia leads to avoidance behaviour. To bring them out of hiding, use the following questions:

- What do you tell yourself will happen
  if you come into contact with your
  feared object or situation?
- What do you believe to be true about
  your phobic stimulus?

Have a look at the following examples of answers
that people have given about their phobias.

*1. What do you tell yourself will happen if you
come into contact with your feared object or
situation?*

- I will become hysterical and embarrass
  myself.
- I will have nightmares about it for
  nights afterwards.
- I will physically shudder and feel sick.

2. What do you believe to be true about the nature of your phobic stimulus?

- Birds seem to know I am scared of them and do things deliberately to target me.
- The few times I have travelled in an elevator it malfunctions. It is as if I somehow cause this to happen.
- Dogs smell fear and therefore can smell me a mile away.

As we have seen, phobic thoughts are not based on fact, which is why these answers may seem illogical, even crazy. The answers above are only a short list of examples, and you may have many more phobic thoughts than this. Make sure you write them all down. If your answers are similarly illogical, then that's great news. It shows you have uncovered your *real* phobic thoughts.

There may be part of you that cringes at the thought of even labelling phobic thoughts. If this is the case, it shows your phobic thoughts are in action at this very moment, lowering your self-confidence. One way to boost your confidence is to use a positive coping statement.

How to use a positive coping statement

A positive coping statement is a sentence that reinforces your belief that you can handle your phobia. It's like a mantra, increasing your self-confidence so that you can label your phobic thoughts without reacting to them.

Your positive coping statement should be personally believable and easy to remember. This prepares you for your phobic thoughts, so that you will not panic or send your mind into a total blank. Having a simple coping statement is like a shield to protect you when emotions become intense.

Examples of positive coping statements that people have used against their phobic thoughts are:

- 'I am stronger than my phobic thoughts.'
- 'I can handle this discomfort, it will soon pass.'
- 'I won't hurt you if you don't hurt me.' [good for animal phobias]
- 'Discomfort means I am unlearning my phobia.'

Take your time to develop a positive coping statement that is uniquely yours. Some people imagine what their favourite action hero or movie star would say if they were in a similar situation. Remember, no one else has to know your positive coping statement except you.

Now it's time to practise labelling your phobic thoughts in a controlled but emotionally charged practice situation. To do this you will need to face your phobia *in your mind*, a psychological technique called visualisation.

Visualising your phobia

Our brains sometimes cannot differentiate between real and imagined events. This is why we react so strongly to nightmares, dreams and even day-dreaming. Have you ever been reading a book, waiting at a red light in your car or listening to a friend, only to lose track of what you were doing because your mind was busily reliving some past event or imagining what could happen in the future? If you have, then it is likely your imagination took over and you were visualising.

When done correctly, visualisation can trick the mind into thinking that it has performed the imagined task in real life. Athletes, musicians and actors are renowned for taking advantage of the power of visualisation when preparing for a major event.

See yourself facing your phobia by doing whatever it is you are afraid of. For example, if you are claustrophobic and scared of travelling in an elevator, visualise yourself calmly walking over to the elevator, pressing the button to summon it, waiting for the doors to open, stepping in, watching the doors close, pressing the button for the next floor, feeling the sensation in your stomach as the elevator rises, and then stepping out at your destination.

Tips for effective visualisation

1. **Visualise in the first person.**

   Always imagine the thing you are afraid of as if you were looking at it through your own eyes. Do not see yourself in the third person as if you were an actor on a movie screen, because your mind will see it as someone else, not as you, reducing the effects of visualisation.

2. **Sit with discomfort.**

   When you feel uncomfortable, instead of abandoning the visualisation, sit with the image and hence the discomfort until it starts to drop. Constantly rate your discomfort using the Phobia Fear Scale you learned in Chapter 4 – it will increase your awareness of your discomfort level dropping. Also use your positive coping statement, 'This will pass' or whatever, to help you through.

3. **Take small steps.**

   If you find the discomfort too intense, break down the visualisation into parts. Spend time becoming calm, looking at the elevator from the outside, then pressing the button, then watching the doors open, then entering it, etc. Go at your own pace.

4. **Remember to breathe.**

   Before you begin to visualise your phobia, remember to take calm, deep breaths. Often when phobic thoughts take hold, the fear will make us forget to breathe properly and we'll either breathe too quickly (hyperventilate) or not breathe at all (hold our breath). Breathing will be discussed further in Chapter 8.

Exercises

1. Practise visualising your phobia

Find a comfortable place with no noise or distractions. If possible, lock yourself away so that you will not be interrupted by others. Sit comfortably in a chair or lie down on the bed or lounge. Remember to take deep, slow breaths and settle yourself. Now, close your eyes and imagine yourself gradually facing whatever it is that scares you. The moment you identify your phobic thoughts speaking, label them. Imagine putting a big label across each one, 'Phobic Thought'. If you experience discomfort during this exercise, rate it, knowing it will soon pass. Go at your own pace, but do it now.

How did you go? Were you able to visualise your phobic stimulus? If you felt a lot of discomfort in doing so, then this is both good and normal. The discomfort shows that you were able to connect with your phobia. Well done! Sitting with this discomfort and riding it out will make it drop quickly. Were you also able to identify and label your phobic thoughts? If you were, that's great. The more you can get to know these thoughts, the more they will be stretched and weakened.

If the visualisation got too much and you had to stop, then that's fine too. Take your time. Keep persevering. Have a break for 10 minutes and then try again.(If you leave it too long before trying again, such as a week, then your avoidance will have strengthened your phobia. Your aim is to make progress, even the smallest amount.) Try visualising with your eyes open; this will make the experience less intense. When you have mastered that, visualise with your eyes closed.

Increase the amount of time you spend visualising your phobia, eventually building up to 10 minutes a sitting or until the discomfort is no longer an issue. To get to this point, practise at least once a day. If done properly on a daily basis, you'll notice a dramatic drop in your discomfort levels within a week.

The more you can face your phobia in your mind, the more you will become aware of your phobic thoughts, and the faster you will become at labelling them – bringing them out into the open and weakening them.

2. Practise using your positive coping statement

Do something small that makes you uncomfortable or is a bit scary. It can be totally unrelated to your phobia, such as walking into a shop you wouldn't normally browse in; driving with your car windows down if you always have them up; wearing a colour or item of clothing that you don't often wear; or taking a different route home. Just make sure it is something you feel you can achieve. While facing this small fear, practise using your positive coping statement and notice the affect it has on your confidence levels.

7

Recruit a phobia friend

Noelene had a phobia of any medical
procedure that involved looking into her
mouth. She avoided using dental floss, as the
possibility of cutting her gums was too
hideous to think about. Dentists were off
limits, even when it meant suffering severe
toothache. One day Noelene developed a
problem with her throat and her local doctor
referred her to a throat specialist. On three
separate occasions, Noelene phoned on the
morning of her appointment and cancelled.
I asked Noelene if she could take a support

111

person with her for the next appointment to see the throat specialist. Noelene was adamant, 'No! I am not a child. I should be able to do this by myself.'

Phobias are very personal and often we do not want to share them with others because, like Noelene, we think we're weak and should be able to get over them. Besides, if we learned our phobia by ourselves then it makes perfect sense to fix it by ourselves too, right?

WRONG!

When preparing to face your phobia, the biggest obstacle will be temporarily forgetting what you have learned and reacting automatically. People with phobias often claim that when they face their phobia, their minds go blank and all they can think about is escaping. To avoid this helpless feeling, you are going to learn how to call upon a phobia friend.

A phobia friend is a trusted support person who is there to motivate you. Think of them as insurance against a brain freeze! They are there to remind you of the steps you need to take, and to help you stay focused when phobic thoughts try to get you to run.

Why share your phobia?

Talking about your fears and worries with a trusted person is the first step to good mental health. The saying 'A problem shared is a problem halved' is especially true when fixing phobias. A phobia friend will help you by:

- Acting as a role model, showing you how to face your phobia.
- Encouraging you and supporting you so your motivation levels stay high.
- Keeping you focused on the steps for fixing your phobia.
- Assisting with managing troublesome phobic thoughts.
- Collecting the necessary phobia props for your 90-minute treatment.

Why is it so hard to ask for help?

Asking someone for help to face a phobia is not easy. It requires trust, something we are not born with, but must learn.

> Charles worked as a storeman at a large manufacturing warehouse. One day his boss asked him to stop what he was doing and help move some containers to the third floor using the elevator. Charles summoned all his courage, took a deep breath and told his boss that he could not travel in elevators as they made him feel uneasy. The boss looked at Charles like he was joking, and then told Charles that people use the elevator every day, and to start thinking positively and just do it. With this, Charles's boss turned and walked away.

Being dismissed offhandedly after baring his soul reduced the likelihood of Charles ever asking someone to help him face his phobia. If your initial experience with disclosing your phobia has been distressing, then it will be more difficult to ask someone else for help. However, this does not have to be permanent. Remember, the degree to which you trust others has been learned. Therefore, given the right situation with the right person, you can learn to trust again.

The main factor that prevents people from trusting others is fear of rejection. We are predisposed to worry about what others think of us – it is humans' Number 1 fear. Being worried about what people think of you is difficult to ignore. The best way to manage this fear is to notice it and accept it as normal. This will help prevent you from beating yourself up mentally and emotionally.

Choosing your phobia friend

A phobia friend can be male or female, young or old, a family member or a friend. They just need to meet three important criteria:

- They can be trusted.
- They are prepared to *learn* to be a phobia friend.
- They are available and accessible.

Where to look

Where do you look for a person with these qualities? A good starting point is the people closest to you.

Partner or family member: Your partner, sibling or parent can make a great phobia friend because they know you well and hopefully have your best interests at heart. Issues that may prevent a family member or partner being a suitable phobia friend are: they may have a similar phobia to you, they do not live close by, they want to rescue instead of support you, or your personalities may clash. Added to this, it is often family members who unknowingly help to keep a person's phobia alive.

Friend: A close friend can make an ideal phobia friend because they care about you, yet are distanced from your family dynamics. However, it might be hard to find someone who is not too busy with their own commitments.

Work colleague: A colleague can be a good phobia friend because they are not emotionally involved in your life. Just make sure that you feel comfortable sharing your phobia with them, and that you can trust them.

Acquaintance: This is someone you know by name, and may have met a few times, but don't know personally. They could be a neighbour, a friend of a friend, or a member of a local group you belong to. If you can establish trust, they can be a useful phobia friend because of their emotional distance.

Is your phobia friend right for you?
It's important that you can trust your phobia friend to take your phobia seriously, and not use

it against you as a source of amusement. I recommend that you get your phobia friend to read this chapter, especially the 'Phobia Friend's Checklist' on pages 83–84. A phobia friend should *not*:

- Laugh and make fun of your phobia.
- Treat your phobia like it is an act and expect you to just get over it.
- Ridicule you in order to motivate you.
- Use logic to try to talk away your phobia.
- Be unrealistic with your treatment.
- Force you into facing your phobia.
- Try to rescue you from your phobia.

If your phobia friend does any of the above, it can make your phobia even worse. This is because your focus will be on protecting yourself not only from your phobia, but also from your so-called phobia friend. Even rescuers, who think they are being helpful, can be harmful. A phobia friend who tries to protect you from feeling fear is forcing you to avoid your phobia, and as you

know, avoidance is the key ingredient that keeps a
phobia alive.

> Patricia tried using her husband as a phobia
> friend. The problem was that the moment
> Patricia's husband saw her discomfort in
> response to her phobia, he started
> questioning the treatment. It was not long
> before he wanted to stop the treatment
> altogether and said, 'You are too old to be
> putting your body under this stress. Besides,
> you have lived your whole life without facing
> your phobia. Let it go.' Patricia's husband was
> trying to rescue Patricia from her phobia.
> However, he was actually trying to rescue
> himself from the discomfort of seeing his wife
> experiencing discomfort.

Be warned: a phobia friend who
cannot sit with their own discomfort in
response to your treatment will sabotage
your treatment every time.

A great way to find out whether someone would make a good phobia friend is to first ask them if they know anything about phobias. If the person puts down the idea of phobias or says something negative about you having one, then be on your guard. However, if the person sounds sympathetic then you may have found yourself a phobia friend.

The next step is to ask yourself some questions about your potential phobia friend. Answer yes or no to the following:

- Do you feel you can trust this person?
- Is this person supportive and understanding of your phobia (i.e. not critical or dismissive)?
- Is this person capable of being a role model (i.e. actually facing the situation or thing that *you* are afraid of)?
- Would this person allow you to face your phobia at your own pace?
- Would this person feel comfortable watching you surf your own

discomfort (i.e. not try to stop you from facing your phobia because *they* feel uncomfortable)?

- Would this person be patient and calm during treatment?
- Do you think this person would be willing to learn how to be a phobia friend?

How did you go? If you answered 'No' to any of the questions (especially No. 3), there's a good chance you might need to choose someone else to be your phobia friend. But before you start looking for someone else, remember that people may respond negatively to an idea they don't know enough about. If you feel they could become the right person, show them the questionnaire on page 80, and then take them through the Phobia Friend's Checklist to educate them about phobias and how a support person should behave. If there is no change in their attitude, find someone else.

*People might respond negatively to the idea
of phobias because they lack information.*

What to expect from your phobia friend

Before you begin treatment, remember that you'll
both be feeling apprehensive: you will be fearful
about facing your phobia, and your friend will be
worried about being able to help you properly. It's
completely normal for your phobia friend to have
negative thoughts and to question whether they
are the best person for the job. It shows they care
enough to want the best for you.

To help put your phobia friend's mind at ease,
explain that even the longest held and strongest
phobias will respond to the 90-minute treatment.
You can also reassure them about what will *not*
happen to you during treatment. Tell them:

- I will *not* die from fear.
- My discomfort levels will *not* rise
  indefinitely.

- Psychological scarring will *not* occur (as long as I follow the correct steps).

It is essential that your phobia friend concentrates on keeping control of *their own reaction* to your discomfort. If your phobia friend looks calm and together, then the effect will be contagious and help instil confidence in you to keep on with the process of facing your phobia. This all comes from your phobia friend focusing on controlling their own reaction instead of yours.

A phobia friend must focus on controlling their own reaction instead of yours.

What's in it for them?

By helping you face your phobia, your friend will:

- Feel good about having helped you.
- Learn about phobias and how to treat them.
- Learn how to help other people face challenges.

- Develop a better understanding of human psychology.
- Learn powerful psychological techniques to use in their own lives.

Phobia Friend's Checklist

You and your phobia friend need to know this list well. I recommend that your phobia friend carries a shortened version (a note with the eight headings) to act as a prompt in case they forget what to do.

1. **Be a role model.**
   During the treatment, whenever the person is ready to take another step closer to the object/situation they are afraid of, it will be *you* taking the first step, with them following your lead.

2. **Help them use their coping statement.**
   Remind the person to use the coping statement they developed in Chapter 6 – it will

boost their confidence to continue facing their phobia.

3. **Help them identify and label phobic thoughts.**

Do this by constantly asking the person what they are thinking. When the person mentions something that sounds like a phobic thought, label it for them by saying, 'That sounds like a phobic thought.'

4. **Remind them to rate discomfort levels.**

Keep reminding the person to sit with their discomfort, to surf it (see page 35), and ask them to rate it using the Phobia Fear Scale. Do this regularly, as it provides proof that discomfort levels are dropping, and that they are beating their phobia.

NOTE: It is normal for discomfort levels to temporarily increase with each step towards a phobic stimulus, and then drop again. Do not take another step closer until discomfort levels have dropped to five or below.

---

5. **Check their heart rate** (optional).

   If the person wants to use a heart-rate monitor (see Chapter 9), remind them to check it
   regularly. When their heart rate drops or
   stabilises, it is physical evidence that they are
   learning to cope.

6. **Offer encouragement.**

   Praise the person when they rate their discomfort and label their phobic thoughts. Even if it
   seems to you that no progress is being made,
   *as long as the person is not running away, they
   are beating their phobia.* Especially encourage
   them to observe their phobic stimulus.

7. **Be patient.**

   Believe in the treatment. It works. At times
   you may begin to doubt it (particularly if the
   person's discomfort levels do not seem to be
   lowering – another reason to use the heart-
   rate monitor which will provide proof that
   their heart rate is dropping, even if they still

seem anxious), but remain focused and positive so that you can be a good role model.
The discomfort *will* drop, sometimes quite
suddenly.

8. **Remind them to breathe.**
    Encourage the person to breathe deeply and
    slowly. You'll probably have to do this often.
    (For more about breathing, see Chapter 8.)

What if I can't find a phobia friend?

Don't worry if you can't recruit a phobia friend.
I will be your phobia friend! I won't be there
in person, but you'll hear my voice. Go to
www.fearispower.com.au and download an
audio file that you can play on an MP3 player to
guide you through your 90-minute treatment.
The website also contains detailed instructions for
gaining maximum benefit from me as your audio
phobia friend.

Listening to me on headphones is obviously not the same as having a real-life phobia friend present, but it is far superior to facing your phobia alone. If you have a phobia friend, I recommend that they download the audio file anyway and listen to it for guidance on how to react during treatment.

Exercise

If you are finding it difficult to share your phobia with someone, then share a small fear first. It can be anything: getting old, watching crime shows on television or listening to the news. That way, as your confidence increases, you can build up to sharing your phobia.

8

Surf your panic

Luke had a phobia of the dark, and being trapped in a dark room was his greatest fear. On his wedding anniversary he decided to take his wife out for dinner to a fancy restaurant. As the waiter led them to their table, Luke was horrified to see that it was situated in a small corner at the back of the restaurant, dimly lit by a single candle. Luke tried to concentrate on the meal, but he found himself constantly looking for the nearest exit. His heart began to beat faster, his hands started shaking, his mouth became dry and his head felt fuzzy. Luke tried to stop his panic, but he could feel his fear of the dark taking control. He had to get out. Luke leapt up and walked quickly to the door. His phobia had won yet again, placing a considerable strain on his marriage.

Panic attacks can make your body feel like it is being pushed to the limit. Indeed, people often fear their panic attack as much as their phobic stimulus. With all this stress on the body, especially the heart, there's a good chance you can have a heart attack, right?

WRONG!

You *cannot* die from a panic attack. Many people end up in hospital emergency departments thinking they are dying or going crazy, when in fact they are simply having a panic attack.

What is a panic attack?

A panic attack is a short period of intense fear or discomfort that comes on quickly in response to perceived danger or impending doom, thereby creating an urge to escape. A panic attack is accompanied by at least four of the following symptoms and feelings:

- Racing heart
- Sweating
- Shaking
- Difficulty breathing, shortness of breath
- Choking sensation
- Tightness or pain in the chest
- Nausea
- Dizziness, feeling faint
- Feeling detached or hyper-real
- Feeling that you're going crazy
- Numbness or tingling
- Chills or hot flushes

NOTE: If you have any heart condition (e.g. angina, high blood pressure) it would be best to have a full medical check-up with your doctor before undertaking the exposure in Chapter 10. This is not meant to give you an excuse not to face your phobia, just to ensure that you do it safely.

Phobias are renowned for causing panic attacks, but, of course, panic is not restricted to phobias. Panic is a fear response to any perceived danger, including everyday situations such as:

- Suddenly realising you have lost your wallet/purse.
- Getting to the checkout and finding you do not have enough money in your account to pay for the groceries.
- Discovering that you have slept in on the day of an important meeting.
- Being pulled over by the police.

Many people mismanage panic by trying to get rid of it, either consciously or unconsciously. Yet the more you try to get rid of your panic by ignoring it, hiding it or trying to subdue the symptoms, the worse it will become.

Mary, a successful business executive, had a phobia of confined spaces. One day in a business meeting, the door to the boardroom malfunctioned and could only be opened from the outside. Mary and her work colleagues were locked in the room, but it was no big deal because they simply had to phone the receptionist in the foyer to open the door. However, Mary felt her panic taking control. She tried to stop it, but her breathing became faster, her chest tightened and her heart began pounding. Perspiring madly, Mary began to feel dizzy. As she tried hard to ignore her panic and hide it from everyone else, it just kept building. Eventually she could not hide it any longer and burst into tears, pleading to be let out of the room. Everyone looked at her in complete surprise. Moments later the door was opened and the problem was solved. However, for Mary it was too late. She felt humiliated and worried that this display of 'weakness' would tarnish her career.

The more you try to get rid of panic,
the worse it gets.

How to manage panic

So if you cannot ignore panic, how do you
manage it? You stop fighting it and ride it out.
Think of your panic like a wave – strong at the
start, but the longer you ride it the weaker it gets,
until eventually it is a ripple on the shore.

To master this, you will first learn to surf *without* the wave – in other words, experience similar
feelings of panic without actually facing your
phobia. One simple technique will make your surfing experience more bearable – deep breathing.

Deep breathing

When it comes time to face your phobia, there
is a chance that your mind may shut down in
response to an overload of phobic thoughts. Deep
breathing oxygenates the blood and keeps the
brain alert so that you can keep your mind
focused and your phobic thoughts contained.

Your aim is to breathe from the pit of your
stomach instead of your upper chest. It can be
practised while standing, sitting or lying down.

The easiest position for learning the breathing technique for the first time is lying down. Later you can practise it while stopped at traffic lights, standing in a queue, watching television, doing jobs around the house or at work.

- Place one hand on your chest and the other hand on your abdomen so that your middle finger is across your navel.
- Inhale slowly and deeply through your nose into the bottom or lowest point of your lungs. Your chest and shoulders should hardly move, while your stomach should rise, pushing your hand out. (If the hand on your chest moves, you are breathing incorrectly.) If the hand on your stomach rises with each inhalation, but the hand on your chest remains stationary, then you are breathing properly.

- When you have inhaled fully, pause for
  about three seconds and then exhale
  fully through your mouth or nose.

Try to breathe in for a count of three seconds,
hold for three seconds, and then breathe out for
a count of three. This is all done using your
diaphragm instead of your chest muscles – simple,
yet very effective. Practise this deep-breathing
exercise whenever you have the chance. Gradually, aim to increase the duration of each phase
from three to four seconds and so on. The more
you practise it, the more it will become automatic. Also see the surfing discomfort exercise on
page 99.

Deep breathing helps keep panic attacks
contained so you can focus on
facing your phobia.

Panic surfing exercises

Try each of the following four exercises to help pinpoint specific body sensations that most resemble the panic you feel when faced with your phobia. When you have found the exercise or exercises that best simulate your panic symptoms, I encourage you to practise them for five minutes, *three times a day*. This will familiarise you with the feelings and thereby lower the panic sensations. Remember, surf the discomfort until it passes.

> NOTE: If you have any medical conditions that you think may be aggravated by the following exercises, seek medical advice before performing them. Do them in an open area where you will not risk bumping into anything if you happen to stumble.

1. *Hyperventilation exercise*

- Take short, sharp, shallow breaths in and out through your mouth as quickly as you can for 30 seconds. This exercise can trigger panic-like symptoms (dizziness, pins and

needles, numbness, seeing stars, dry
mouth or tight muscles).
- After 30 seconds, revert to the deep-
breathing technique you learned
above and surf the discomfort until it
passes.
- After 10 seconds of deep breathing,
most of the symptoms will have
receded.

2. *Dizziness exercise*
- Sit in a swivel chair or stand with your
hands straight out at your sides,
parallel to the floor.
- Spin around in circles 10 times. Then
stand as still as you can. You will feel a
rush of dizziness set in.
- Surf the discomfort and notice both
how the dizziness is not harmful and
how it settles very quickly.

3. Light-headedness exercise

- Sit in a chair and put your head between your knees, hanging your hands down next to your feet.
- Stay in this position for 30 seconds, then jump up quickly. You will feel light-headed, perhaps even as though you might faint.
- Surf the discomfort until it settles. It will only be a matter of seconds until you notice your head clearing.

> NOTE: If you have heart trouble, consult your doctor before doing the following exercise. If you have injured knees or legs and cannot run, try push-ups or lifting light weights with your hands for a similar amount of time to increase your heart rate.

4. Palpitations exercise

- Depending on your fitness level, walk or run up a flight of stairs, or step on and off a small step from 30 seconds to a minute. Notice your rapid heart beat.

- Surf the discomfort using deep
  breathing. Notice how your heart rate
  soon normalises.

What if I faint?

Some people with a blood or needle phobia may
faint in response to their phobic stimulus. They
may go to extreme measures to avoid it, reducing
the safety and quality of life of themselves and of
those around them. They may:

- Never go to the doctor or dentist.
- Be unable to care for children (or
  adults) who have hurt themselves.
- Never watch the news, TV programs
  or movies where they may see blood.
- Be unable to walk near the meat
  section in a supermarket.
- Faint if they overhear someone else
  talk about blood.

It is unusual for people with other types of phobias to faint in response to encountering their phobia.

> Barbara had a phobia of blood. While at work, she overheard one of her colleagues describing how they'd been out to dinner and ordered a steak that arrived undercooked. When this person cut into the steak, blood poured out of it. Upon hearing this, Barbara felt woozy and fainted on the lunch-room floor. An ambulance was called. Barbara was assessed and declared fine. The medics, however, could not do anything for Barbara's embarrassment.

NOTE: If you faint in response to your phobia, first have a medical check done by your doctor to make sure it is your phobia triggering this response.

Why do I faint?

Your brain is above your heart, yet gravity pulls your blood towards your feet. For blood to reach your brain and other organs (i.e. effective circulation), it is pumped under pressure. Two factors maintain your blood pressure: 1) the smooth muscle in your blood vessels, and 2) your heart rate. When the blood vessel walls contract, less blood can flow through, thereby increasing the pressure. When the blood vessels relax, there is more room for the blood to move. When your heart beats faster, more blood is pumped through. But if the heart suddenly slows down, less blood is pumped through.

Fainting is controlled by the vagus nerve in your nervous system. When the nerve is stimulated by pain, fear or other distress such as the sight of blood, the heart beats more slowly and the blood vessel walls relax. This results in blood pressure dropping and blood pooling towards your feet. Your brain is starved of oxygenated blood and you start to feel light-headed and/or dizzy. When you faint, your brain is then at the same level as the blood in your feet. Fainting is a radical method the brain uses to restore blood flow.

Phobias of blood, injury and injections where fainting occurs result in your heart slowing down. This is in direct contrast to all other phobias, which result in your heart speeding up so you can escape perceived danger. Psychologists have many theories, but they still do not understand the evolutionary benefit of humans fainting in response to the sight of blood. One theory is that it is our version of 'playing dead' to avoid attack, and another is that lowering blood pressure minimises bleeding from an injury. It is also interesting to note that even though phobias are learned, research suggests that some people may have inherited a hypersensitive vagus nerve from their parents.

How do I prevent fainting?
Fainting occurs because your heart slows and your blood pressure drops. To prevent the fainting response, you are going to learn to do the opposite and become active. When certain muscles are tensed in a specific way, blood cannot be pulled

down towards your legs and instead is directed to the muscles at work.

The anti-fainting exercise below is designed to keep the blood moving in your body and should be practised five times a day for at least a week before facing your phobia if you have a blood, needle or injury phobia. The exercise does not involve anything strenuous. Instead, you will be required to tense your muscles. Tensing large muscles increases blood pressure sufficiently to prevent fainting.

Exercises

1. **Anti-fainting exercise**

   Sit in a quiet and comfortable place where you can be alone and free from distraction. Use slow, deep breathing throughout the exercise. Concentrate on the muscles in your legs, arms and abdomen. Now tense these muscles and hold the contraction until you feel a rush or warm feeling in your head. This usually occurs after about 10 to 15 seconds, but may take up to 30 seconds. Remember to keep breathing, and do not tense your head, neck or face.

If you have trouble feeling this warmth in your head, keep trying for up to five times, have a break for 30 minutes, and then try again.

When you do feel the warmth in your head, hold it for 10 to 15 seconds. Then relax for 30 seconds.

Now repeat the contraction, holding and rest process five times. Do this exercise fives times a day – this would make twenty-five contractions throughout the day. Even though this may seem like a lot of work, the more you practise, the better you will be at applying it in the real world.

2. Surfing discomfort exercise

Take a normal drinking straw and cut a quarter off it. Place this small section of the straw between your lips and breathe normally so air only goes in and out through the straw. At first you may have panicky feelings of suffocation. Surf the discomfort and continue to use slow deep breaths. The discomfort will drop. This is also a great way to master deep breathing.

> **NOTE:** If you develop headaches from the anti-fainting exercise then you are probably using the muscles in your shoulders, neck or jaws. Remember, you should only be tensing your limbs and abdominals. If the headaches still persist, cut back on the intensity of your contractions, and if that doesn't work, consult your doctor.

9

Small steps

Now that you have read the previous eight chapters and practised the associated exercises over a period of weeks, you're probably feeling a little impatient to get the 90-minute exposure over and done with. After all, if the way to fix a phobia is by confronting it, you may as well get it over with quickly and face it head-on, right?

WRONG!

Even though the head-on method can work for some people with phobias, the risk of it strengthening the phobia is far too great. Remember, confidence is a fragile thing. Therefore, it is in your best interests to approach your phobia with care from the start.

There are many advantages to facing your phobia in a planned, systematic way rather than jumping in at the deep end:

- You will become accustomed to feeling fear gradually (in smaller, more manageable amounts).
- You will minimise the chance of failure.
- You will strengthen your confidence.
- You can gain a sense of control over the treatment process.
- You will reduce the risk of unwanted surprises during treatment.

Your 'exposure plan' describes the steps and equipment involved in conquering your phobia. *You* are in control of your exposure plan because you will be the one who designs it. You are the boss of:

- When you do the exposure.
- Where you do the exposure.
- How quickly you take the steps.
- When the exposure ends.

Having a systematic exposure plan that you have personally designed is important for confidence, especially when phobic thoughts start creeping in, trying to convince you that treatment will not work. Remember, *you are the boss of your treatment plan*. It is important that nobody, including your phobia friend, forces you to do anything that you have not already agreed to do prior to starting treatment.

If you are still having reservations about facing your phobia and wondering if there is an easier way, rest assured that this is normal. These concerns are your phobic thoughts talking. Try to remember that if there were an easier way to conquer your phobia, you would have already done it. The only proven method of overcoming a phobia is to be exposed to it in some form.

Even though the thought of facing your phobia may be uncomfortable, the anticipated discomfort is often much worse than the experience of actually confronting your phobia. The whole aim with exposure is to learn to feel in control of yourself, instead of feeling like your phobia is in control of you.

The best way to develop this feeling of self-control is by taking small, planned steps towards your phobia. As the old saying goes, 'A journey starts with a single step.' In order to foster this self-control, you first need to know what you want to achieve in facing your phobia.

Avoid unrealistic expectations

When designing a phobia exposure plan, people often fall into the trap of thinking too big. That is, they think that if they face the worst possible situation then they will defeat their phobia for good. This gives rise to foolhardy ideas for exposure such as:

- Jumping overboard when way out at sea to fix a phobia of water.
- Being locked in a coffin to treat a phobia of confined spaces.
- Sitting in a bath with dozens of slugs to beat a phobia of slugs.

This type of thinking is nonsense and potentially harmful. Even people without phobias would find these situations challenging.

Remember, developing a sense of mastery over your reaction will allow you to conquer your phobia.

Shane had a phobia of heights and took an unrealistic step to try to beat it: he went parachuting. It sounded like a good idea at the time, but unfortunately, after the jump, Shane still could not climb a ladder to change a light-bulb.

So why did Shane's treatment fail? Because jumping out of a plane in no way simulated his phobia in everyday life, and it also empowered Shane's phobic thoughts by begging the obvious question, 'You can jump out of a plane, but can you climb a ladder?' Do not be fooled into thinking that your first step in facing your phobia has to be a huge one.

Know where you want to go

It is essential to set a specific goal and then plan for it to happen. As the saying goes, 'By failing to plan, you are planning to fail.' Your specific goal should reflect the *final stage* of your phobia exposure plan. For example:

Phobia	Possible ultimate goals
Animal/insect	Be in the same room as the creature Touch a cage/box containing the creature Touch the actual animal/insect
Confined spaces	Ride in an elevator Travel on a train, plane or bus Be in a crowded place such as a theatre

Phobia	Possible ultimate goals
Height phobia	Walk over a bridge Climb up a ladder Stand close to the edge of a lookout
Water phobia	Travel on a ferry Swim in a pool or the ocean Take a bath
Needle phobia	Give blood Have a needle at the dentist Get a flu injection

Knowing the *final stage* of your phobia exposure plan allows you to then work backwards and design the different steps leading up to it. If you are having trouble coming up with this final stage (because your phobic thoughts prevent you from even contemplating the idea), then ask yourself this question: 'How would my life be different if my phobia was conquered?'

- Shelley, who has a dog phobia, said she would be able to visit friends who had dogs so long as the dogs were restrained.

- Mark, who has a height phobia, said he would be able to apply for jobs where the interviews were conducted in offices above the ground floor.
- Sally, who has a phobia of water, said she would be able to take her kids swimming at the local pool.

Make your exposure plan

Now that you have identified the final stage in facing your phobia, you can develop an exposure plan or 'ladder', where you work out the steps you will take to get there. The way to gauge the difficulty level of each new step is by rating your discomfort levels on the Phobia Fear Scale from Chapter 4. Make sure they gradually increase in intensity.

Depending on your phobia, you will need some props that trigger your phobic response. Ideally, each step should involve facing a new phobia prop that is slightly more challenging than the last. For example, in the case of a spider phobia, phobia props might range from a cartoon picture of a spider to a real spider in a jar (this is where your phobia friend is invaluable, as they can be in charge of collecting props for you).

Below is an example of an exposure ladder, including phobia props, where each stage is rated on the Phobia Fear Scale.

Exposure plan for a spider phobia

Step	Situation	Fear Scale Rating
1	Look at a photo of a spider	5
2	Touch the photo of the spider	6
3	Watch movie footage of a spider	7
4	Touch a rubber spider	$7\frac{1}{2}$
5	Touch a dead spider	8
6	Be in the room with a non-poisonous spider that is contained in a jar	9
7	Capture a live, non-poisonous spider and release it outside	10

I recommend having five to eight steps in your exposure plan. Too many steps can reinforce avoidance so that you lose confidence and enthusiasm and your phobia wins. Conversely, too few steps will mean each stage has to be more intense, making it harder to conquer your phobia.

For some phobias, a new step might not involve new props – it could simply be your distance from your phobic stimulus. For example, a person with a phobia of heights may have a final stage of wanting to be able to stand out on the balcony of a two-storey house and look down over the balcony rail at the ground.

Exposure plan for a height phobia

Step	Situation	Fear Scale Rating
1	Stand in the living room and look out towards the balcony rail (10 metres away)	5
2	Walk to the doorway out to the balcony (6 metres from the balcony rail)	6

Step	Situation	Fear Scale Rating
3	Place one foot on the balcony and look out towards the horizon (or a distant landmark), keeping the other foot in the house	7½
4	Walk up to the balcony rail and place one hand on it, holding your phobia friend's arm with the other hand; keep looking at the distant landmark	8½
5	Place both hands on the balcony rail and keep looking at the distant landmark	9
6	Shift your gaze to an object/ landmark that is closer and requires you to tilt your head down a little bit	9½
7	Shift your gaze again, slowly, until you are looking straight down over the balcony rail	10

The time you spend at each step will vary. Often the longest time will be spent sitting and waiting for the discomfort to drop on the first and final stages. I have treated some people who have spent over 30 minutes on either the first or last step, yet sped through the others. Taking this into account, the general rule for determining the time spent between steps is to divide 90 by the number of steps in your exposure plan. If you have eight steps, then aim at spending around 10 minutes per step. If you go overtime on any of the steps, arrange beforehand with your phobia friend to try to make up time on subsequent steps. Your phobia friend will be your time-keeper, which will help motivate you to stick to the 90 minutes.

> A word of caution: Your phobia friend is there to motivate you, not to force you to do something you do not want to do. *Ultimately it must be your decision to take that next step.*

For more examples of exposure ladders for different phobias, go to www.fearispower.com.au.

Preparing for your 90-minute exposure

1. Find a location

Where is the best place to face your phobia? Will
it be indoors or outdoors? Can it be done at your
own or a friend's home, or will it require going
to a specific location? Try to find a location that
isn't crowded with people as this can cause
distractions. For example:

Phobia	Examples of locations
Height	Bridge, second-storey balcony, fenced scenic lookout
Animal	Zoo, pet shop, friend's home
Needle/blood	Your own home with a trained person who can administer the needle, or if organised beforehand, a blood bank, medical centre, hospital
Water	Beach, swimming pool, ferry, boat ride
Confined spaces	Elevator (preferably where there are not too many people around), tunnel, subway, home or other venue with a closet or basement

If you are having trouble simulating your phobic stimulus (e.g. flying in an aeroplane, thunder, lightning or storms), see 'Treatment challenges' on page 112.

2. Collect your phobia props

A phobia prop (e.g. pictures, video or movie footage, plastic replicas) should be able to trigger a phobic response. It is important that props invoke fear responses of varied intensity so they can be used in setting up your exposure plan.

Phobia	Prop examples
Spiders	Plastic spider
Vomit	Fake vomit
Injections	A syringe
Storms	Sound effects CD with a storm

If you are unable to collect the props yourself, have your phobia friend gather or organise the appropriate phobia props you require for exposure.

3. Confirm your phobia friend

Ask your phobia friend to commit to the treatment date you both set. Having a phobia friend
cancel the night before can lower your confidence
and willingness to treat your phobia in the future.
Confirm that your phobia friend has their checklist ready to follow on the day, or make one for
them and bring it along.

If you do not have a phobia friend, ensure
you have downloaded my cyber phobia friend
(**www.fearispower.com.au**), an instructional file
that talks you through facing your phobia. You
will need to have a portable audio playing unit,
such as an MP3 player with headphones, so that
you can listen to the download while facing your
phobia.

4. Get a clock/watch

Use a clock/watch to keep track of time. Sticking to
the 90 minutes becomes a goal in itself and acts as
a motivator. This is vital, especially when phobic
thoughts subtly tell you to procrastinate about

taking that next small, planned step towards your phobia. Have your phobia friend act as time-keeper.

5. *Consider getting a heart-rate monitor*

A heart-rate monitor is a simple device that straps around your chest under clothing and transmits a signal to a little device you wear on your wrist. It's a fantastic aid, as it will show you that your heart and body are coping with your phobic stimulus long before your mind realises that you are. As you see your heart rate dropping, your confidence builds and helps to weaken your phobic thoughts.

What to Expect

To maintain a sense of control when facing your phobia, it helps to know that it is normal to experience any of the following:

- **Second thoughts:**
  It's normal to feel apprehensive and
  to want to back out at the last

minute. This is simply your phobic thoughts talking – they will come up with any excuse to prevent you facing your phobia, such as having a mild cold, sore throat, headache or a bad night's sleep. Unless you have to go to hospital, go ahead with the treatment. Adrenaline will kick in to help on the day.

- **Heart rate increase:**
Whenever you take a planned step closer to your phobic stimulus, your heart rate will increase, but it will come back down reasonably quickly too. You'll see this clearly if you use a heart-rate monitor.

- **Dizziness:**
Dizziness is often a sign that you are breathing incorrectly, so breathe deeply. In the case of blood and needle phobias, make sure you do your anti-fainting exercise. You have

learned both deep breathing and anti-
fainting exercises in Chapter 8.

- **Other physical reactions:**
Sweating, dry mouth, butterflies
and/or nausea, or the need to go to
the toilet are just some of the ways
your body will be preparing itself to
face your phobic stimulus. This is fear.
Welcome it, because fear primes your
body so you will perform at your best.

- **Racing mind:**
Your mind will race and may even go
blank. Once again, this is normal.
Breathe slowly and deeply to take
back control of your response so you
can focus on conquering your phobia.

- **Visual avoidance:**
For some people, as soon as they see
their phobia there will be a strong
desire to look away. Force yourself to
keep looking at your phobia and surf
the discomfort. As you learned

through your exercises in Chapter 8,
the discomfort will drop very quickly.

- **Remember:**
Whenever you take a planned step
closer to your phobic stimulus,
discomfort will temporarily increase,
but then drop quickly within a few
minutes. Accept the discomfort as
normal and surf it out until it drops.

Treatment challenges

What happens if you try to face your phobia but
things do not go to plan? There are a few reasons
that this might happen.

Choosing an inappropriate phobia friend

If your phobia friend is not properly educated in
how to help you face your phobia, then they may
put you off with their own discomfort, or may
be unsupportive and push you into a situation
you do not want to face, stripping away your

control. Make sure they have read Chapter 7 and reinforce what is expected of them before you start treatment.

Forgetting to label phobic thoughts

Your phobic thoughts will try to make you terminate treatment at every chance. Phobic thoughts need to be identified and handled correctly – see Chapter 6.

Taking too big a step

Going too fast because of impatience or being pushed into taking too big a step too quickly will take away your sense of control. This risks strengthening your phobia, as does having a poorly planned exposure ladder.

Leaving too quickly

You must sit with your discomfort at each new step for a realistic amount of time until the discomfort has dropped to five or below. If you terminate treatment before your discomfort drops

to an acceptable level, then you risk strengthening
your phobia.

Selecting a poor location

Choosing an inappropriate location will prevent
you from concentrating fully on your phobia. For
example, conducting your exposure with people
everywhere may be distracting and make you self-
conscious. Likewise, a location without a safe exit
will lower your self-confidence.

Choosing the wrong phobia props

Choosing phobia props that are inappropriate will
only serve to reinforce your phobia. For example:
selecting an animal that is not placid or not securely
contained; selecting a photo or video footage that
is too extreme (such as the movie *Arachnophobia*);
choosing a needle that a health professional would-
n't ever use. Even though it is recommended that
your phobia friend be responsible for physically
collecting your phobia props, make sure that you
are involved in the selection process.

Difficulty accessing your phobic stimulus
Some people have difficulty accessing the situation or thing that triggers their phobia. Fear of flying and natural environment–based phobias (fear of lightning, thunder or storms) can be difficult to access, so you need to be creative. Some options could be:

- **Use audiovisual material** for natural-environment phobias (e.g. a recording of a storm; a movie with lightning footage).
- **Target the phobia that is most present and/or easiest to access** (see Chapter 2). In the case of a flying phobia, for example, some people are fearful of heights, others of being in the confined space of an aeroplane cabin and still others are afraid that the plane will crash. By fixing the phobia that is easiest to treat, you can use the confidence and skills learned

to target the more difficult one
(i.e. taking a flight).

- **Face your phobia in your mind
  with visualisation** as discussed in
  Chapter 6. Even though direct
  exposure is best, indirect exposure
  through visualisation is a good
  alternative.

Exercises

1. **Plan your reward**

   Decide how you will reward yourself after
   facing your phobia. Choose something really
   special. Remember, fixing your phobia is a
   major achievement, so make sure you do
   reward yourself – rewarded behaviour gets
   repeated.

2. **Run through your checklist**
   - Exposure ladder/plan
   - Phobia props

- Location
- Heart-rate monitor (optional)
- Phobia friend (who has read the checklist on pages 83–84)
- A copy of your checklist written out for your phobia friend
- Agreed time and date with your phobia friend
- Timer
- What to expect (re-read pages 110–111)
- Planned reward

10
Victory!

Once you have successfully treated your phobia, you might think it is best to put it behind you and move on. After all, regularly thinking about your phobia shows that you have not moved on and may actually cause it to become strong again, right?

WRONG!

To discard your phobia after it has been fixed is a bit like throwing away a tool box after completing a repair job. Being crippled by a phobia for years and then successfully facing it in 90 minutes is a *rare, life-changing experience*. By conquering your phobia you have learned to stay in control of yourself in a fearful situation. Many people run the moment they even come close to feeling fear. But you have learned to surf discomfort – an amazing skill that you can apply in other areas of your life, such as:

- Asking the boss for a raise, or time off from work.
- Starting or ending a relationship.
- Changing direction in your working life.
- Joining a new hobby group, enrolling in a class or starting a new sport.
- Saying 'No' to others.
- Dealing with something you have been putting off.

However, self-control is not the only skill you have learned in the process of overcoming your phobia – you have also learned:

- How to acknowledge and work on a major issue in your life.

- How to analyse a challenge by breaking it down into smaller and more manageable stages.
- How to be patient when taking small, planned steps (even though your instinct is to rush and get it over with).
- How to identify and manage unhelpful thoughts.
- How to select and recruit a suitable support person(s) for assistance.
- How courageous and determined you are!

These skills, derived from fixing your phobia, have placed you in a powerful position to tackle other fear-provoking challenges. Below is an example of an exposure plan for managing the fear associated with giving a speech at a wedding.

Exposure plan for giving a speech at a wedding

Step	Situation	Fear Scale Rating
1	Write the speech out on paper	4

2	Practise the speech out loud with no one present	$4\frac{1}{2}$
3	Practise the speech alone in front of the mirror	5
4	Practise the speech and record on a video camera	$6\frac{1}{2}$
5	Give the speech in front of your support person	8
6	Give the speech in front of a small trusted group of family/friends (no more than five)	9
7	Give the speech at the wedding	10

Just as you did in treating your phobia, the aim is to take small, planned steps so that you:

- Become accustomed to feeling fear in gradual amounts so that you can develop a sense of control over your reaction.
- Become aware of your thinking to determine whether it is unhelpful or not.

- Notice how fear is making your body react.

You could use a similar plan for facing your fear of job interviews, giving a public performance or travelling to new destinations.

What about more complicated fears?

Giving a speech is the kind of activity that can be broken down into steps. But what about fears that seem less straightforward and more spontaneous, such as managing cravings for food, cigarettes or alcohol, dealing with difficult people or saying 'No'? For these situations you will use the powerful technique of surfing discomfort. Facing your phobia has taught you to focus on *controlling your own reaction* rather than controlling the fearful situation, and resisting the impulse to flee. Knowing you can sit with discomfort and surf it out until it drops can be applied to numerous situations in life. For example, next time someone asks you to do something, even if you are happy to do it, instead of immediately replying 'Yes', surf the discomfort and say that you will think about it and let them know later.

The more you practise applying what you have learned to other challenges in your life, the easier it will be to overcome them. You will be using your phobia's unique strength as a springboard to empowerment to change your life for the better!

Exercise

As a final exercise, share your newfound knowledge and become a phobia friend for someone else who has a phobia. A fixed phobia is a gift, and a gift is meant to be shared. Share yours.

Acknowledgements

Thanks to Jonathan Dyer, the driving force behind this book. I'm indebted to you for all the hours you have put in helping create this book. You are a gifted writer, editor and an amazing friend.

Thanks to my lovely wife, Mel, without whose loving support this book would never have been possible, and to my beautiful children, Emma and Patrick. I'm very proud to be your dad.

Thanks must also go to my agent, Sally Bird, from Calidris Literary Agency, who worked tirelessly to find me a publisher; to Kirsten Abbott from Penguin, for her support and belief in the book and to Miriam Cannell from Penguin, whose professional editing skills have refined the book and taken it to a whole new level.

Special thanks to my parents, Ron and Helen, who have always been there for me; to my parents-in-law, Bruce and Cynthya, for their support, enthusiasm and love; to Ian my brother, you're one in a million; to my sister Kazz and her husband, Adrian, and my nephew Zack, for believing in me; to my brother Mick and his family Leanne, Ben, Jade and Mitchell; to my amazing grandmother, Marie Thorold; to David Thorold, my 'Uncle D' in New Guinea; and my cousins Ollie, Ron and Mary Anne – thanks for all your support with my writing career.

Thanks also to Ron and Dee Karney, who took me under their wing and helped me find my way in life when I was going through difficult times; to Kylie from Handprint Photography, for her great photos; to Aunty Anne, who'll be in my heart forever; to Uncle Neil, and Brent and Sarah – it was fun growing up with you all.

Finally, thanks must go to Jennifer Harold and Elizabeth Williamson, and all the clients I have worked with over the years, for their great courage in overcoming their phobias and for teaching me so much.